T0165283

Praise for Suzanne Beecher's *Muffins & Mayhem*

"Beecher is an inspiring entrepreneur, and she relates the details of her unusual life with candor."

—*Library Journal*

"Suzanne Beecher has lived a colorful, tragic, wonderful life, which she chronicles in *Muffins & Mayhem*."

—*Chicago Tribune*

"[T]hose hoping for charming tales of after-school cupcakes or Rockwellian family dinners will be in for a surprise."

—*Publishers Weekly*

"From the first laugh to the last tear, Suzanne had me in her thrall. Part memoir, part cookbook, part comedic romp, this is a book written with candor, bravery, and soul on every single page."

—M. J. Rose, internationally bestselling author of *The Memorist*

"Loved, loved, loved it! Reading *Muffins & Mayhem* was like a visit with your BFF, sitting at the kitchen table over a pot of tea and chocolate-chip cookies, sharing secrets, shedding tears, and laughing. Always laughing!"

—Barbara Bretton, *USA Today* bestselling author of *Laced with Magic*

"What a brilliant little gem of a book! Like a recipe for life, alternately heartwarming, funny, touching, and inspiring, Suzanne Beecher's unique voice comes shining through. If you want to learn how to live your life with passion and joy, read this book, right now."

—Nate Kenyon, author of *The Reach* and *Sparrow Rock* (and devoted DearReader fan)

How did these people do it? How could they remember all of these things? And what the heck was wrong with me, that I couldn't?

So I took a quick inventory and discovered my one-dimensional childhood consisted of these four scintillatingly dramatic "stories":

1. I was born in Madison, Wisconsin. We didn't live there—we lived seventy-five miles away, in the small town of Cuba City, population 2,000—but my mother became very ill in the last six weeks of her pregnancy, so the doctor sent her to the big-city Madison hospital.

2. My parents and I lived in a trailer for a while—just long enough to save up money for a down payment on a house.

3. I had a green dress with a scratchy cancan slip underneath it. I think this was in the fourth grade.

4. When I was in eighth grade, the first round school building in the county (maybe even the state) was built in Cuba City. In the middle of the school year, we all packed up the stuff in our old desks and walked in a single-file pilgrimage from the old rectangular school building to the new round one.

The End

That's the short, happy childhood of Suzanne Beecher in 157 words, plain and simple. And boring, even to me.

So I accepted my fate as an adult deprived of a childhood. Or at the very least an adult deprived of those warm and fuzzy memories I should have been able to tap into when I wanted to go back home in my mind. But then it occurred to me that I'd always been ambivalent about going home anyway—not only in my mind, but in my car, too. At least it seemed that way. Whenever I planned a trip to see my parents, I'd get sick. I'm not kidding! Two or three days before I was supposed to leave, an illness would consume me: wheezing, sneezing, that all-over crummy feeling. Nothing serious, a twenty-four-hour virus sort of thing—but just enough "miserable" so I'd have to cancel my trip. My recovery period was amazing. And eventually I realized there was a pattern: As soon as the "magic hour" had passed and it was too late to go, no hope of getting back home in time for a weekend visit, I was cured.

So I asked myself: Really, what's the big deal? Who cares if I can't remember any cute childhood stories—didn't want to go back to measly podunk Cuba City, anyway. It was a stupid town, one of those blink-and-you'll-miss-it dots on the map. Cuba City meant nothing to me. My life is all about what happens to me now. Right?

But then Mrs. Creswick died. She was my girlfriend's mother. Everyone called her Purse, but I never used her nickname, or her real name, Priscilla. It seemed more respectful to address her as Mrs. Creswick.

When I heard the news that Mrs. Creswick had died, I realized I'd lost something precious from my past. Every kid needs a role model, and although I hadn't realized it at the time, Mrs. Creswick was one of mine.

I loved going to Mrs. Creswick's house because she made me feel special. She always made sure there was cottage cheese and those little cherry tomatoes in the refrigerator because she knew I loved them. Course I don't really know for sure—I was just a kid. Maybe she always had cottage cheese and tomatoes in the fridge—but she knew they were my favorite, so she'd set a plate in front of me every time I visited.

Mrs. Creswick was a great cook, and there was love in her kitchen. Whenever I got the chance, I liked to watch her make dinner. One afternoon she even taught me how to make her famous Frosted Meat Loaf. When I asked for a copy of the recipe, she helped me write it down on one of her recipe cards, along with personal tips on how not to burn the meat loaf when it was time to put it under the broiler. I still have the faded Frosted Meat Loaf recipe card today.

It was important for me to let someone know how special Mrs. Creswick had been to me. So I called her husband and my old girlfriend, gave them my condolences, and shared my childhood memory of the Frosted Meat Loaf. Then I dug out my old recipe card and started cooking. Mrs. Creswick would have been proud of me, because her Frosted Meat Loaf came out of the broiler just right.

Years ago I'm sure Mrs. Creswick thought she was simply giving me a recipe for meat loaf, and for a long time that's what I thought, too. But suddenly it was all so clear—the things that make me what I am today, the things I really like about myself, they all came from growing up in Cuba City. Remember the girl who was ambivalent about going home? Mrs. Creswick's meat loaf finally showed her the way.

So if a plate of cherry tomatoes and cottage cheese and a Frosted Meat Loaf recipe could leave such a big impression on my heart, maybe there were other little things in my life that I was overlooking?

I'm a daily columnist who writes about life, and after I wrote the story about Mrs. Creswick's Meat Loaf the tone of my columns changed. I guess what really happened is I wasn't afraid to open my heart and let readers see the real me. Now I freely write about the feelings I wrestle with every day—my father's final farewell apology, embarrassing moments like the day I was trying to make a big impression but suddenly realized a lint roller was stuck to my behind, trapping Mighty Roach in the middle of the night, and how I couldn't get back in the groove after my mother died even though we'd never been close.

When I opened up my heart to readers, they opened up their hearts to me. Hundreds of people email every day and tell me their stories. In fact, one woman's email, another Priscilla, inspired me to write this book. . . .

Dear Suzanne,

I have been following your Dear Reader column for several years now. I am so grateful you are willing to share with your readers a glimpse of your life, whether it's happy or sad.

Let me introduce myself: I am a 43-year-old mother of three children ages 8, 10, and 11. I have been diagnosed with late-stage metastasized lung cancer.

Knowing that I won't have the privilege of walking my three young children through their tough teenage years and adulthood, I want to prepare a scrapbook for each of them to fall back on when they are down and have no one else to turn to. When I was reading your column about the "writing inspiration" folder you keep, it strikes me to the core—that's exactly what I want to prepare for my kids. Something to inspire them to be the best person they possibly can, and to pick their spirits up on a rainy day when things feel out of control and they need to get themselves grounded again.

It will be greatly appreciated if you can share some pointers with me as to where to find these inspiring books, articles, quotes, etc. Thank you for your time!

Yours sincerely,
Priscilla

And my reply . . .

Dear Priscilla,

It's always a pleasure to hear from a reader, especially someone who has been reading with me for such a long time.

Some of the most precious things I own are the photo albums and recipe box that my Grandma Hale passed on to me. Whenever I thumb through the albums, or I'm following the recipe on one of Grandma's recipe cards, I feel like she's standing right beside me in the kitchen. It's such a comfort, and the memories come flooding in.

Making scrapbooks or journals you can leave for your children is a wonderful, loving thing to do. They are going to miss you, and you're right, there are going to be sad times in their lives when no one else but their mother could comfort them.

Pictures in a scrapbook with a caption underneath about why this was your favorite, or something about the day the photo was taken—your kids would love the photos. And when you make a list of books that have made a difference in your life, you could explain the reason why.

But Priscilla, I think the most important thing you can tell your children is what you are thinking, or were thinking. Write down what you were thinking on your first date (it doesn't have to be fancy), how it took you hours, maybe days, to figure out what to wear. How awkward your first kiss was. Tell them about the day you flunked your algebra test, how you worried that you might not make it into college, or why you felt you didn't need to go. Why you decided to say yes and get married. How did you meet their father? On days when you feel like a loser, what do you do to get yourself grounded again?

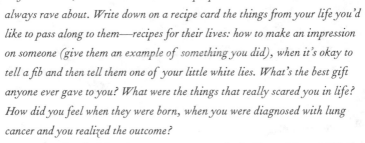

Create recipe boxes for your children and include your favorite recipes and stories. Leave your children a handwritten copy of the recipes for your very best meals, the cake or casserole that people always rave about. Write down on a recipe card the things from your life you'd like to pass along to them—recipes for their lives: how to make an impression on someone (give them an example of something you did), when it's okay to tell a fib and then tell them one of your little white lies. What's the best gift anyone ever gave to you? What were the things that really scared you in life? How did you feel when they were born, when you were diagnosed with lung cancer and you realized the outcome?

My mother died from lung cancer a year and a half ago. My son said that he asked my mother if she was afraid to die. She told him no, that she didn't think it would be quite this soon, but that she wasn't afraid. That statement has brought my son so much comfort. I know, because he's mentioned it to me several times.

There are things I wish I had asked my mother, and most of them begin with "How did you feel about . . . ?"

Don't weigh yourself down with the need to write fancy, just simply write. Pretend your kids are sitting in front of you and start talking. I can picture you leaving each one of your children a recipe box filled with recipes for cooking and recipes for their lives, written on 3 x 5 index cards.

Priscilla, I wish I could say something to make everything better. I'm so sorry. There is a quote I say out loud to myself when it feels like my world is falling apart and I need to get grounded. It always brings me at least a moment's respite. I'm saying it out loud for you today.

"If I knew the way, Priscilla, I'd take you home."

Priscilla did make recipe boxes for her children. Unknowingly, she left a gift behind for me, too. I didn't realize it until I wrote back to Priscilla, but for years I'd been creating my own recipe box, and the stories I discovered in it inspired me to write this book.

I've picked out some of my favorite dishes and recipes from my life—the stories that help keep me grounded in this unpredictable world, like Mrs. Creswick's Meat Loaf. Stories that remind me I'm okay, just the way I am.

Recipes are meant to be exchanged, so please share my book with your friends—and substitutions are allowed. Maybe there's a Mrs. Creswick hidden away in your heart, filed away in your own recipe box? My hope is by the time you're finished reading the recipes from my life, you'll be reliving some of your own, and if you're still looking, I hope you find that missing ingredient.

Mrs. Creswick's Frosted Meat Loaf

It's a one-bowl recipe. I keep a box of light disposable gloves in my kitchen for jobs like mixing a meat loaf. You can use a mixer, but I like to get my hands in the meat loaf. For the frosting, peel a couple of Idaho potatoes, or quickly mix up some instant mashed potatoes.

Meat Loaf

2 pounds hamburger
½ cup French dressing
½ cup dry bread crumbs
½ cup chopped onions
2 eggs
1 teaspoon salt
¼ teaspoon pepper

Meat Loaf Frosting

2 cups hot mashed potatoes
1 egg, beaten
½ cup Miracle Whip

Mix all meat loaf ingredients together. In a baking dish, shape into oval loaf. Bake for one hour at 350 degrees. Then mix frosting ingredients together, and frost meat loaf. Broil until slightly brown.

Introduction

Life isn't always about the serious stuff.

My recipe box gets a lot of use. It's filled with the necessities of life—stories to help keep me grounded and recipes for good stuff to eat, like the Funeral Cake—my favorite cake since I was a kid. I realize that may sound a little strange, but in Cuba City when I was growing up, whenever someone passed away, neighbors would take food over to the bereaved family so they wouldn't have to worry about cooking. Even if they didn't have much of an appetite, most likely there'd be a steady stream of friends and relatives stopping by their house, and this way they could offer their guests something to eat.

I made sure to tag along with my parents when they'd go to drop off a casserole and offer their condolences, because I was hoping to get a piece of the Funeral Cake. It was the absolute best chocolate cake I'd ever eaten and it always showed up at every grieving family's home in Cuba City. And when my mother died five years ago and friends and neighbors brought food over to her house, guess what showed up then, too?

The Funeral Cake.

What a surprise when I discovered that the Funeral Cake baker, the woman who'd been making my favorite cake all those years—a devil's food cake with a light buttercream frosting—was Betty, a shirttail relative of mine.

Frequently I thumb through my recipe box looking for a story to reassure me things are gonna be all right. I have good intentions, but more often than I like to admit, my life gets off course, so I spend a fair amount of time "fixing" myself. My feelings change daily, sometimes hour by hour. Blame it on a headache, blame it on some bad fish I ate for dinner, blame it on not getting enough sleep, or the hormones I'm juggling in this phase of my life called menopause, but one minute I'm a happy camper, and the next, I'm wondering what went wrong—isn't it time to take a nap?

Other days are amazing, and I'm certain I've finally found the perfect recipe for my life. Happy and contented, creative beyond my wildest dreams—things are cooking now—but I'll wake up the next morning and for some reason see myself on the cover of *Loser* magazine and it'll be time to get out my recipe box again. Time to find a recipe to assure me that even though things don't look promising at the moment, this is the recipe I followed in the past when life got scary but everything turned out fine.

I'm a complicated person, even to me. It's embarrassing to admit, but I spend a lot of time wondering *why*. I might wake up in the middle of the night trying to come up with possible reasons why the supermarket clerk kept giving me nasty looks when she was ringing up my order. I suppose it would be easier for me to figure out why I bother spending time wondering about such things and work on changing *me* instead.

But through the years, I've come to realize that I'll never be able to completely rid myself of that particular personality trait, and I'm not so sure I'd even want to. Because it's not always the "bad stuff" I review later on in my mind—I learn a lot from taking another look at the "good stuff," too. When I'm in the middle of a daily interaction, the little cues, mannerisms, and words that someone chooses might slip right by me. It happens all so fast. But when I think about the encounter later in the day and I write about it, visualizing and replaying how it all went down, I learn a lot about me.

The recipes from my life, each story teaches me something about myself. For example, this one reminds me why I don't always need to be the best.

The woman down the street is one of those wonderful people who is always planning something fun, and I say that with all sincerity, because I'd probably be a social recluse if it weren't for her invitations. So when she invited me to a neighborhood bake-off, I RSVP'd "yes." The only instructions: Be ready to serve by 6:30 p.m., and whatever you bring to the bake-off, make sure it contains chocolate or berries.

Knowing my neighbor as I do, calling it a "bake-off" could simply be her clever ruse for getting people to bake for her, because she's not a baker. Was there really going to be a first prize, or a judge, for that matter? Just in case, I decided to make Lava Cakes, which are best right out of the oven when the warm, gooey chocolate is running out of the center. It was a risky choice because of the timing, but they're impressive and they taste divine. My plan was to put the Lava Cakes in the oven at 6:10, bake them for thirteen minutes, and then head to the party. (My neighbor's house is only a three-minute walk away.)

I was thinking I should probably be feeling a little nervous, because when you're baking something at the last minute, there are no second chances. I might have had to show up empty handed, but surprisingly it didn't bother me, and that was a wonderful realization.

It's not that I don't usually lean toward risky choices, I do. In fact, some people would say that's part of my trademark. But in the past, whether

I acknowledged it or not, there was always a backup plan waiting in the wings—all the details worked out in advance, checked and double-checked, even for something as trivial as baking Lava Cakes. But this new loosey-goosey approach, I liked it. I think I could get used to feeling like this. There *was* a bake-off judge and a first-prize blue ribbon, but I didn't win it. A chocolate dessert that didn't require delicate timing came in first. You really need to eat Lava Cakes right out of the oven, so I came in an easy-going second—and it was quite all right with me.

Life isn't all about the serious stuff. When I need a good laugh—when I'm looking for the "funny" in life—I can find those stories in my recipe box, too. Here's one of my favorites.

I couldn't see clearly because I didn't have my glasses on and it was the middle of the night. But I was pretty sure that the big, blotchy mass running up the wall next to my bed wasn't there when I went to sleep.

Lights on!

Yell at husband! (He's in charge of things that scurry in the night.)

Pull covers over my head! (In case the blotchy thing goes airborne.)

Yes, we have an exterminator. But every now and then a critter gets through the outside bug barrier, as this roach—a really big roach—obviously did. He was bold, all right. He knew we'd seen him; he could have retreated, but he chose to stay put and defend his wall. Okay, this was war!

My husband's weapon of choice was a rolled-up newspaper, but I quickly reminded him that squishing the enemy on the wall would make for a messy cleanup job, possibly even touch-up painting. I suggested the vacuum cleaner instead. And after a fleeting chase, the vacuum did indeed suck that roach right up through the hose. Now safe and secure, I thought I'd drift right off to sleep. But I didn't.

Did you ever watch the *Mighty Mouse* cartoon show when you were a kid? I did, and for some reason the image of Mighty Mouse with his chest puffed out, flexing the muscles in his arms, was suddenly crystal clear in my mind. Now all I could think about was, *What if that roach spends all night in that vacuum cleaner bag, munching on yesterday's toast crumbs, and in the morning he crawls down the vacuum hose and emerges as Mighty Roach? He's not gonna be too happy.*

Lights on—again. Yell at husband—again: "You hold the vacuum cleaner hose upright, dear. I'll get the duct tape."

Yes, life is definitely entertaining at our house. My husband says he married me because he knew life with me would never be boring. I don't intend to let him down.

The Funeral Cake with Buttercream Frosting

½ cup vegetable shortening
1½ cups sugar
1 egg
½ cup milk
2 cups all-purpose flour
2 teaspoons baking soda
½ teaspoon salt
½ cup cocoa
1 cup boiling water
1 teaspoon pure vanilla extract

Cream shortening and sugar. Mix in the egg. Add the milk, alternating with the following ingredients that have been sifted together: flour, baking soda, salt, and cocoa. Stir in boiling water and vanilla. Bake at 350 degrees (grease and flour pans).

Loaf pan 13 X 9 X 2: 40 minutes
Two round 9-inch pans for a layer cake: 30 minutes
Cupcakes: 17 minutes

Buttercream Frosting

If you're making a layer cake, double this frosting recipe.

½ cup milk
2 tablespoons all-purpose flour
1 stick soft butter
½ cup granulated sugar

Mix together milk and flour. Cook over medium-high heat, stirring constantly until thick, then let the mixture cool. Cream together soft butter and sugar. Then whip the milk and butter mixtures together. Frost your cake or cupcakes and enjoy!

Suzanne's Lava Cakes

Makes 6 cakes

These cakes look very impressive, but they are super simple to make. I love them. I like to serve them with a scoop of vanilla ice cream on the side.

6 ounces bittersweet chocolate, chopped
10 tablespoons butter
1 teaspoon pure vanilla extract
3 large eggs
3 large egg yolks
1¼ cups powdered sugar, sifted
½ cup all-purpose flour

Preheat the oven to 450 degrees if you are baking the Lava Cakes immediately. Butter six ¾-cup ceramic ramekins.

Stir chocolate and butter together in medium saucepan over low heat. Stir in vanilla. Cool the mixture slightly. Whisk eggs, yolks, and sugar together in a large bowl. Add chocolate mixture and flour. Pour mixture into the prepared ramekins, dividing equally. Cover and chill if you're making the Lava Cakes a day in advance.

Bake cakes until the sides are set, but the center remains soft, about 11 minutes. (If you refrigerated the batter, you might have to bake them for up to 15 minutes.) You really do want the center soft and runny on the inside, so remove the cakes from the oven promptly—and don't second-guess yourself.

Immediately run a small knife around the edges to loosen the cakes. Then invert each cake onto a single serving plate.

1. A Budding Chef

Grandpa Hale built the kitchen cupboard for me, and that's my dog, Moochie, sitting on the floor hoping I'll spill.

I learned how to cook when I was eight years old and singing backup for the Monkees.

Mom and Dad worked every day, including Saturdays, and I was an only child, so the weekend chores were left to me. Every Saturday morning, before my mom left for work, she'd tape a list on the front of the refrigerator.

Susan, (my given name)

1. *Iron*
2. *Vacuum the living room and bedrooms*
3. *Dust everything*

4. *Clean the bathroom*
5. *Fix lunch*

NO playing outdoors until your work is done.

Love, Mom

I'd always get the work done, at least most of the time. But the "getting-it-done" part didn't start until about an hour and a half before my parents came home for lunch, because I'd get sidetracked by other important things. Like lip-synching with the Monkees.

Hey, hey, we're the Monkees
And people say we monkey around.

A bottle of Pledge was my microphone and a pair of my mother's high heels gave me that onstage look. I'd draw the curtains over the big picture window in our living room—I wasn't ready for an audience yet—then I'd slide back the cover of our dark wooden console stereo, put the Monkees' 33⅓ LP on the changer, click the switch, and when the needle dropped the magic would begin.

Sing a few tunes, then take a break to do a little dusting, pound the round steak—Swiss steak was on my lunch menu—brown the meat, add some onions and tomato sauce, and pop it in the oven just in time to do another set with the Monkees.

Timing is everything when you're onstage, and when you're cooking, too. If the backup "doo-wops" come in on the wrong beat, the song is ruined. If the meat doesn't have enough time to slow cook, it won't turn out fork-tender. Everything has a rhythm to it: peel the potatoes, set them aside; vacuum the floor, then open a can of peas and dump them into a saucepan—but they'll have to wait for their cue to start cooking because it's time to go back onstage.

Thirty minutes left before lunchtime: put the potatoes on medium-high; tilt the lid over the saucepan to let some of the steam out; set the table. Only fifteen minutes left: Open the drapes, turn down the music, take one last look around the house, and by the time my parents walk through the door, Mike, Davy, Mickey, Peter, and I have finished two curtain calls—our last number was "Forget That Girl"—and I'm in the kitchen smiling and stirring the peas when I hear the front door open.

"Hi, Mom, hi, Dad, lunch is ready."

Cooking was the one thing I seemed to do right when I was a kid. My parents never came right out and said, "Wow, that was a great meal, Susan," but they ate it and sometimes even went back for seconds, so it was implied that I'd done a good job.

But when other people tasted my Porcupine Meatballs at the church picnic and raved about what a good little cook I was, I believed them. And when the neighbor down the street asked me—just a kid in elementary school—if I would give her my recipe, I felt proud as a peacock. So even though making lunch started out as another dreaded chore on my Saturday list, cooking was something I really got to like doing—a "safe" hobby. Something I could be proud of.

I had to choose hobbies carefully when I was a kid, because my mother's rule was if you started something you were going to finish it. Even when I went to the library I only checked out thin books—just in case. So a hobby like knitting was totally out of the question. What if something went terribly wrong? From past experience I knew the routine—there wouldn't be any such thing as a practice, *learning-how-to-knit* sweater. If I tried to make a sweater, it wouldn't matter if there were twisted stitches, or if it ended up two sizes too big—I'd be wearing it to school anyway. "I paid good money for that yarn. You'll grow into it."

It was bad enough that I had to wear the jumper I made in home economics class to school. My wide-ribbed, dark green, corduroy jumper was cut from the same pattern as everybody else's. So even if I'd actually liked the stupid jumper, no way did I want to wear it to school. It would have been a fashion disgrace. Think about it—all twenty girls in my class showing up for school wearing a rainbow assortment of corduroy jumpers, all cut from the same pattern, on the same day? I don't think so.

But cooking was different. If my timing was off—if I did too many curtain calls to "I'm a Believer"—I could hide my mistake with a can of cream of mushroom soup. Cut the burnt part off the fried chicken, throw the dried-out meat into a casserole dish, mix a can of cream of mushroom soup with milk, pour it over the chicken, salt, pepper, then sprinkle half a can of French's French Fried Onions on top and instantly it was chicken casserole.

Cream of mushroom soup saved me from the taste of burnt chicken and ketchup saved me from the taste of liver. My mother didn't like to cook and it showed. Once every two weeks—at least!—she served liver. It was frightening. As soon as I saw Mom slicing up that big slab of liver into little liver servings, and dipping them in flour and heating up the oil—I got on the phone and started calling friends as fast as my fingers could dial.

"Have you eaten yet? Can I come over for dinner? I just got *Sgt. Pepper's Lonely Hearts Club Band* and I'll bring it along. You can even keep it for a week. Please? I really need to come to dinner."

If those calls didn't produce a liver reprieve, I'd plead with our neighbor to get off the party line, so I could start dialing friends of friends. "Hello there, I'm Ginger's best friend and she thought we should get to know each other. Have you eaten yet? By the way, I just got the new Beatles album. . . ."

Mom liked liver because it was cheap. It didn't matter that I hated the stuff. "This isn't a restaurant, I'm not a short-order cook." And of course the other half of that sentence was something about not wasting food and my mother's hard-earned money. So I had to sit at the dinner table until I ate every single bit of the liver and onions piled on the plate in front of me. Oh, did I forget to mention the onions? Not that they made the dinner any more palatable. The onions were cooked in the same pan as the liver.

Gagging produced no sympathy at the liver dinner table. My only salvation was ketchup. Dump lots and lots of ketchup on the liver, pinch my nose with two fingers, then shove as big of a piece of liver as I could get down my throat without choking, while listening to my mother lecture me on the cathartic "truths" of eating liver.

When my mother got a "truth" about something in her head, like liver, even if you could absolutely, positively, prove it not to be true—it didn't matter. Her truths were absolute. And my mother had a truism about ironing, too. Everything in our house that touched our bodies needed to be ironed, including socks, sheets, pillowcases, and even underwear. Why? "Because I said so."

I never understood the logic of it all, but I did it. Wash the clothes, roll them up while they're still wet, and freeze them—yes! Freeze them, even in the summer! So instead of playing softball on Saturday, it was my job to unroll those frozen stiffs and iron the wrinkles out of them.

Why didn't we just dry the clothes? Because my mother said it cost too much to run the dryer. And she even defended that "truth" when she had to buy a second freezer. The small freezer on the top part of our refrigerator didn't have enough space for the frozen peas and my dad's underwear, too! So Mom bought a new upright freezer and put it in the basement, and all we kept in it were our frozen clothes.

Wash the clothes, roll them up, freeze in the wrinkles, and buy a freezer whose only purpose was to freeze the sheets? Sounded crazy to me. But hey, I was just a kid—what did I know?

Old habits die hard, and I confess that today I continue to iron some of my clothes and pillowcases, too. And yes, if the sheets come out of the dryer with too many wrinkles I give them the once-over. But ever since I moved out of my parents' home, I'm proud to say I've never ironed anyone's frozen underwear.

Porcupine Meatballs

Serves 4

1 pound ground beef
½ cup uncooked instant rice
½ cup water
⅓ cup chopped onion
1 teaspoon salt
½ teaspoon celery salt
⅛ teaspoon garlic powder
⅛ teaspoon pepper
1 (15-ounce) can tomato sauce
1 cup water
2 teaspoons Worcestershire sauce

Preheat oven to 350 degrees. Mix meat, rice, ½ cup water, onion, salts, garlic powder, and pepper. Shape mixture into meatballs. Place meatballs in ungreased baking pan. Stir remaining ingredients together and pour over meatballs.

Cover and bake for 45 minutes. Uncover and bake 15 minutes longer.

Dresses, bows in my hair, ankle socks, and patent leather shoes, I loved to get dressed up. Clothes were definitely this girl's best friend when I was growing up.

It was a blessing and a curse and it sat right smack in the middle of Main Street. Everybody knew it as the Dime Store, but it was really called The Ben Franklin Store. My mother worked there when I was a kid. Today, whenever I see an old Ben Franklin Store I have to go inside, because to me it feels like home. Truth is, if it hadn't been for the Dime Store I never would have gotten to know much about my mother.

Mom wasn't much of a talker. When she did speak up, she rarely started a sentence with "I feel . . ." But after school when I'd stop by the Dime Store to say hi, I got to see the way my mother felt about something—her job. Work was the thing Mom did best. At the Dime Store she was self-assured, very confident in her abilities. But when it was time to go home at the end of the day, I think my mother felt a bit lost and out of place in the world.

Mom started out at the Dime Store as an inexperienced part-time clerk, but by the time she left thirteen years later, my mother *was* the Dime Store, at least in my eyes. Watching my mother all those years instilled in me the confidence that I could accomplish anything if I put my mind to it. If there's a will—and Mom always had plenty—there's a way. I know, because I learned it from my mother.

My favorite memory of Mom is her in the back room of the Dime Store surrounded by stacks and stacks of pink, green, and yellow Easter grass, woven baskets, toy shovels, colored eggs, and candy. She always made up the Easter baskets for the store. I guess when you think about it, my mother was Cuba City's Easter Bunny.

The Dime Store was a blessing not only because it brought me closer to my mother, but also because it acted as Cuba City's whatever-you-needed "general store." And it was an especially great place for me to get school supplies, because I got first pick at everything before Mom put it out on display.

But the Dime Store was my worst nightmare when it came time to buy school clothes. If my mother couldn't buy something at the Dime Store, then in her mind, I didn't need it.

My mother never understood fashion; she only understood her 20 percent employee discount. If I didn't have another store's coupon that matched it, then there was no discussion—the Dime Store's striped, short-sleeved shirt tucked into an A-line cotton skirt was going to be my "chic look" for school in the fall. This all seemed perfectly logical to my mother, because she was a woman for whom nothing in her closet *ever* went out of style.

But the "A-line Dime Store look" wasn't the look I had in mind when I was thumbing through the JCPenney catalog, circling the clothes I had my heart set on wearing. And the Dime Store look certainly wasn't going to impress my friends, either. So I got a babysitting job. Because early on I'd learned the most dependable recipe for getting what I wanted—at least from my mother:

🌀 Work hard, no "ifs, ands, or buts" hard.

🌀 Earn my own money.

🌀 Mix in a little extra housework for Mom on the side; only then would she bend her Dime Store rules.

Babysitting was an easy fifty cents an hour, because the two boys I took care of just wanted to play outside with the other kids in the neighborhood. So after I fixed them lunch and did some light housekeeping for their mother, I spent the rest of the afternoon sitting in the sun with lemon juice in my hair and listening to Neil Diamond. My hair was dark brown, but I desperately wanted to be a blonde, just like Sharon, the girl who lived across the street. Sharon was the reason my boyfriend dumped me, which convinced me that blondes really do have more fun.

My mother didn't care about my boyfriend problems and she wouldn't even discuss the possibility of letting me dye my hair, even though the Dime Store sold hair color. But an article in the June issue of *Teen* magazine came to my rescue. "Brunette and want to be blonde? Sit in the sun with lemon juice in your hair and it will get lighter." But it didn't get any lighter—it just got sticky. Squeezing lemons, singing along with Neil Diamond, *Cracklin' Rosie, get on board*; and secretly wishing something awful would happen to Sharon. It was a long hot summer. But the lemons did give me another moneymaking idea.

SUSAN'S ICE COLD LEMONADE. It was a simple beginning—a card table with a sign taped to the front of it, purple and green aluminum tumblers, and fresh-squeezed lemonade. But after the first day I didn't need the table or the sign any longer, because I learned one of the ingredients of a successful business—networking.

My dad worked as a mechanic at Dellabella's, the local Buick dealership, which was practically in our backyard. The lemonade business was slow because we didn't live on a busy street, but when I took my wares over to the garage where my dad worked, suddenly business was booming. Not only did my dad buy a glass of lemonade, but all of the other mechanics bought some, too. Dad said I couldn't continue to sell lemonade at the garage unless his boss gave the okay, so I mixed up a big glass of lemonade, added a bendy straw, and offered Mr. Dellabella a free sample. By the time I left his office, I'd secured a lemonade contract for the summer. I would be the sole supplier of ice-cold lemonade (twice a week) for all of Mr. Dellabella's mechanics and even for some of his new car-buying customers.

I have only fond memories of my lemonade business. So one day when I was driving around doing errands and I noticed two young entrepreneurs standing behind their lemonade stand, I just had to stop. The girls had a real sense of style and merchandising: bright yellow lemon slices were neatly stacked in a row on a cutting board and tall slender glasses surrounded a pitcher of lemonade in a semicircle. The pitcher was there for show, to whet the appetite. The real stuff was in a cooler, hidden away underneath the fancy lace tablecloth that covered their card table. The girls were even selling "add-ons"—blueberry muffins showcased on top of a real white china plate. Two smiling faces were beaming from behind their "counter" eagerly awaiting customers. So I stopped.

"What a nice stand! How much is your lemonade?"

"Four dollars," one of the girls quickly replied and her business partner chimed in, "and the muffins are three dollars and fifty cents each."

"Four dollars for one glass of lemonade?" I was dumbfounded. *School clothes must cost more than they used to. Four dollars?* I wasn't familiar with this neighborhood, but looking around at the very expensive homes, it was obvious I'd ventured into the high-rent district. This must be the Rodeo Drive version of a lemonade stand. *Four dollars?!* I wasn't even sure I had that much cash on me. It never occurred to me that a sentimental stop at a kids' lemonade stand would send me in search of an ATM.

When I was a kid, the going rate for a glass of lemonade was ten cents plus the occasional tip. But combined with the money I earned from baby-sitting, it was enough to order some of the JCPenney clothes I'd circled in the catalog. And whatever I couldn't afford, I'd borrow from my friends, especially when I needed an outfit for the Saturday night dance.

Almost every other weekend a live band played in the Cuba City school gymnasium—pretty amazing entertainment for a town of 2,000 people. Teenagers from the surrounding small towns, like Benton, Dickeyville, and Hazel Green, came to the dance, too. So I guess that's how they were able to sell enough tickets to pay for the band. When you're a kid, you don't think about those nasty profit-and-loss concerns. Instead, I worried about important stuff, like what I was going to wear to the dance.

It always took me at least a week of trying on clothes to find the perfect outfit. Because after I tried on everything in my closet I'd look in my friends' closets, too, and that's where I found it—in Judy Gallagher's closet. It was perfect for the dance: a square-necked, sleeveless, brown and yellow polka-dotted dress shorter than anything I owned, or had ever worn. It would never pass the school knee-length-or-longer dress test—they made you get down on your knees and if the bottom of your skirt didn't touch the floor, the principal sent you home to change. But this dress was the perfect length for the dance—I would definitely get noticed.

Unfortunately I got noticed *before* the dance. Judy brought the dress over to my house so I could try it on, and that's when my mother walked by and saw us dancing in the full-length mirror.

"Just where did you get *that* dress?" My mother seemed upset.

"Oh, it's not *my* dress, it's Judy's. . . ." but in the middle of trying to explain that Judy was lending me the dress for the dance, my mother had a meltdown and pretty much went berserk right in front of Judy.

"YOU'RE NOT LEAVING THIS HOUSE IN THAT DRESS! YOU LOOK LIKE A HUSSY! WHAT PARENT IN THEIR RIGHT MIND

WOULD EVER LET THEIR DAUGHTER WEAR SUCH A SHORT DRESS?"

"Well, Judy's mother would. She let Judy wear the dress to school last Tuesday." (This was the truth, but not the whole truth. I neglected to mention that Judy was several inches shorter than me.) "Anyway, this isn't a school dress, Mom, it's a dance dress."

"TAKE IT OFF. YOU'RE NOT WEARING THAT DISGUSTING DRESS ANYWHERE—AND THAT'S FINAL!"

Well, okay, I pretty much understood what was going on now. But how do you sort things out when your mother has just embarrassed you in front of your friend, and insinuated that your friend is a "hussy" because she wore *this* dress to school last Tuesday, and that your friend's mother is one of *those* mothers, because she let her daughter wear it?

I was furious with my mother. Judy ran out the front door before I could say anything to her. Mom embarrassing me in front of my friend, and that polka-dotted dress hanging in my closet, they haunted me for the rest of the week. It wasn't fair. My mother just didn't get it. After all, it was only a dress! What harm could come from wearing a polka-dotted dress to the dance?

So instead of going out the front door when I left for the dance Saturday night, I waited until my parents were distracted and then I climbed out my attic bedroom window, onto the roof, where it was only a short jump down to the ground. I brushed myself off, walked across our backyard, crossed over Main Street, and three blocks later I was at the dance, feeling pretty cool in Judy's short polka-dotted dress. My friends and I waited in line to buy our tickets, and when I went to hand my ticket to the man by the entrance—there stood my mother!

It still makes me queasy when I think about it today. My mother didn't say a word. She didn't have to. I knew what was coming and so did my friends. They gave me a commiserating look of sympathy. *Good-bye, so long, it was a nice childhood while it lasted,* because they knew my mother, and they knew I'd probably be grounded for the rest of my life. And it felt like I was. Six weeks later, I finally got to go to another dance. Just to be safe, I wore long pants.

Every year when the first few snowflakes showed up in Cuba City, they sent another horrifying fashion signal to my mother. It was time to get out the snow pants. My mother thought snow pants were functional. My friends and I considered them an embarrassment. No self-respecting, fashion-conscious elementary school girl would wear snow pants. But my mother didn't care. She made me wear them underneath my dress when I walked to school, so my legs wouldn't get cold.

I'd reason and plead with my mother for days about why I didn't need to wear snow pants—and every year I'd lose the argument. So I always did the next best thing. I'd leave the house with the snow pants on underneath my dress, but as soon as I crossed over Main Street, once I was out of sight from our house, I'd duck behind the repair business on the corner, take off the snow pants, fold 'em up, and wedge them in between my books.

Taking off my snow pants wasn't an easy thing to do because the pants wouldn't slip over my rubber boots. So I'd have to take off my boots, then pull off my shoes, take off the snow pants, put my shoes back on, retie them, and then put my rubber boots back on. It was quite a production and when there was snow on the ground, I had to hop on one foot and then the other so my socks wouldn't get wet. I felt pretty silly, but I'd always remind myself that it was my secret. Turns out it wasn't.

Years later when I was visiting my parents for the weekend, Mom had sent me to the grocery store for a couple of things. When I was standing in the produce section I heard someone in the next aisle. "Well, hello there," she said. "You're Virginia and Ernie's girl, aren't you? I remember you, but I wouldn't expect you to remember me."

Good thing, too, because I had absolutely no idea who this woman was.

"I used to live across the street from the repair shop on Main Street," she continued. "Every morning when you were a little girl I'd watch you duck back there and hide your snow pants. You were the cutest thing."

The woman was laughing now, but I wasn't. Even though I was in my thirties, I felt like I'd just been caught.

"It was always kind of sad to see the snow start melting," she said, "because that meant pretty soon your mother wouldn't make you wear snow pants."

I laughed nervously along with her, but I also recognized a familiar tense, worried feeling in my stomach. So I asked if she'd do me a favor.

"I realize I'm all grown up now and that it shouldn't matter," I said, "but could you please not mention this story to my mother the next time you see her?"

Thankfully she agreed.

At least snow pants meant the possibility of a snow day. And whenever there was the slightest chance that a big snowstorm was headed toward Cuba City I'd get up early in the morning, even before my parents, and turn on the local radio station to hear the verdict. It was like Lotto for kids.

"And now for the local school closings," the announcer would finally say.

Okay, this was it. I was hoping, wishing. The listings were in alphabetical order, so Cuba City was always near the top, but I could hardly stand the wait. I'd be down on my knees in front of the radio, practically praying as the announcer got closer to the *C*s.

"Please say it. Come on, come on, you can do it. Let me hear it." Finally the moment I'd been waiting for!

"Cuba City Schools will be . . . *(here it comes: yeah!)* . . . starting two hours late today."

You've got to be kidding! Two crummy extra hours? That was almost worse than going to school on time. Since the bus didn't pick me up and my parents both worked, that meant I'd have to spend part of those two hours wading through snowdrifts—in those stupid snow pants. And if that wasn't bad enough, my mother always added to my misery with one of her lists: "Susan, since you'll be going to school late this morning, vacuum the living room, do the dishes, and change the sheets on the beds before you leave."

Snow or no snow, there was one of those lists waiting for me every day after school, except on Fridays. After school on Fridays I always went right to the Dime Store. And as soon as Mom got off work, we'd meet Dad at the IGA store on Main Street and the three of us would head straight for the frozen-food department. We were on a mission—hurrying to pick out our favorite Swanson TV dinners so we could get home and heat them up before *Rawhide* started.

Mom and Dad ate their dinner on folding trays in the living room with me sitting on the floor between them, balancing my crispy chicken TV dinner on my lap in front of our black-and-white console television. And as soon as the music started and the opening credits started rolling past on the screen, I'd sing along with the theme song:

Keep them doggies rollin', rawhide!

You'd be amazed how often things from my childhood, like *Rawhide*, pop into my head at the weirdest times. A few years ago, when I was in a meeting at a Fortune 500 company, I'd finished my sales presentation and the president wanted to show me a new promotional piece they'd just finished working on. He cued up the video on the big screen and when I heard the accompanying background music, instantly it reminded me of the theme song from *Rawhide*. I couldn't resist telling him about my family's Friday night date with *Rawhide*. It was obvious he was an old *Rawhide* fan—he nodded animatedly as I set the scene. And without giving it a second thought, I started singing the theme song out loud:

Rollin', rollin', rollin' . . .

To my surprise (and I think his, too), after a couple of lines, he started singing right along with me. The other executives sitting around the boardroom were staring at us like we were crazy. But the two of us kept right on singing, and driving those cows home:

Keep them doggies movin', rawhide!

P.S. Yes, I made the sale.

Whenever I go back home to visit Cuba City, one of my favorite things to do is take a walk around town. Last time I invited my husband to come along with me because I wanted to show him some of my favorite places from when I was a kid. But when we were walking the streets and alleys of my hometown, I soon realized my husband was on a different walk than I was.

When we reached my friend Judy's old house, my husband saw paint peeling, duct tape wrapped tightly around an air conditioner in the window, and front porch boards that were rotting. But that's not what the house looked like to me. No peeling paint, no broken shutters in my mind. To me the house that my old friend Judy grew up in—the house that stood before me—was neat as a pin, just the way it looked thirty-five years ago.

The lot down the street is vacant now, but there used to be swings, five in a row, their chains hanging down from tall, steel poles. See the worn spots on the ground underneath the swings? That's where I used to drag my feet. Sometimes I'd go so high in the air it felt like the swing might wrap right around the top of the pole. I'd stretch out my legs, and then pull them back with as much force as a seven-year-old could muster. I was hoping to keep the momentum going just a little bit longer—I was flying. But eventually the swing would start slowing down, and I'd drag the toes of my shoes back and forth on the ground to bring the swing to a final stop.

When my husband and I turned the corner and walked toward Main Street, we saw a commemorative train car for tourists sitting where the train tracks used to run alongside the old post office. I walked those train tracks every day on my way to school. And on the weekends I'd head in the other direction, following the tracks, past the city dump, till I got to the huge mounds of gravel and sand piled high in the middle of nowhere. The perfect place to pretend I was a secret agent.

I worked the Friday Night Fish Fry at the restaurant on the corner of Main Street when I was in junior high. The air conditioner could never keep up with the heat in the kitchen, so we'd always leave the back door open. In between washing dishes, my job was to peel the huge Idaho potatoes and put them, one at a time, in the potato slicer that was bolted on the wall. Then I'd slam the long handle down and freshly cut french fries, with a little bit of peel still left on, would fall into an old white pickle bucket. But one night I miscalculated and my finger got caught in the french-fry cutter and I had to go to the emergency room. That was the bad news. But the owner still paid me for my entire shift, which was the good news, because I was saving to buy my parents a wooden rocking chair for their anniversary. The man at the furniture store on Main Street had it on hold for me.

And walking down another street, the story continues. My husband is admiring the new supermarket, but not me—I'm climbing the old apple tree in Orville Sands's yard instead. Yes, we're walking together hand in hand, but my husband's on Main Street, and me—I'm strolling down Memory Lane.

My Favorite Blueberry Muffins

These won't cost you $3.50 apiece!

I buy fresh blueberries in season and freeze them in a good-quality freezer bag, so I have berries year-round.

Makes 12 muffins

1 cup superfine sugar
½ cup butter
1 cup milk
2 eggs
1⅓ cups all-purpose flour
2 teaspoons baking powder
¾ teaspoon cinnamon
¾ teaspoon nutmeg
½ overflowing teaspoon vanilla extract
¼ teaspoon salt
1 cup fresh blueberries or thawed frozen berries

Preheat oven to 375 degrees.

Using a mixer, cream sugar and butter on low speed until smooth. Add milk, eggs, ⅔ cup of flour, baking powder, cinnamon, nutmeg, vanilla, and salt. Mix just until thoroughly blended. Mix gently, by hand, the remaining ⅔ cup flour and the blueberries. (Batter should still be lumpy.) Fill muffin liners ⅔ full. Muffins will rise one inch. Bake 20 to 30 minutes, until golden brown. Let cool a little bit before serving. (You can double this recipe and it will turn out fine.)

3. Loose Wires

Christmas Eve my parents and I would drive to Grandma and Grandpa Hale's house. Every year Santa would leave new pajamas for me under the tree. My all-time favorite, striped red-and-white jammies with a cap. Yes, I looked ridiculous for a few months, but Grandma believed in growing into things.

For longer than is easy to admit, I walked around with loose wires in my brain. While other teenagers were applying to colleges and planning their futures, I was getting drunk and looking for love in all the wrong places. Some people were quick to blame my parents; instead I used to blame myself. The truth is, Mom and Dad and I were each doing the best we knew how to do. Yes, parents are supposed to know the way, but my parents missed the day they handed out the informational brochure about *How to Love and Raise a Well-Adjusted Child*. (I'm pretty sure *their* parents were absent that day, too.) Mom and Dad didn't intentionally fall down on the job; they simply couldn't give me what they'd never experienced themselves. If they could have freely let go of their love and still survived, I believe they would have.

So where did that leave me? Trying to figure out how to write a successful recipe for my life, a better recipe than the one my parents were using. Common sense told me when you're trying to figure out how to do something better than *before*, you need to take a closer look at *before*. "Learn from your mistakes," advises the old adage, and eventually I did write a new recipe for my life, but it sure was rough going for a while. People seem to be amazed when I find the courage to tell them about the things I did when I was young—young, maybe, but old enough to know better. Some perils are so embarrassing and downright insane, even I shake my head in amazement. What was I thinking?

I don't know for sure, but I am certain I wouldn't go back and change a thing, because even my misguided choices serve me well today. Hopefully the screwed-up scenes in my life help me be less judgmental toward other people. "Why does she stay with that man when he continues to abuse her? How could she make such a stupid choice for her life?" When other folks stand back, roll their eyes and wonder, it's no mystery to me—been there, done that.

By the time I was twenty-two years old I'd already experienced a lot of life, but didn't understand it. I was married when I was sixteen—yeah, I don't know why, either, because when it was time to start walking down the aisle I remember thinking, *I don't want to do this*. But I also knew my folks had paid in advance for the pink and white daisies adorning my bridal bouquet, rented the American Legion Hall (it was a big deal for a small-town wedding), and hired a caterer and a band for the reception, so there was no turning back.

In my mother's eyes when a decision had been made, especially if it involved money, it didn't matter if it didn't quite fit. "You'll grow into it," or "You'll learn to love him," Mom explained the day she informed me I was getting married. End of discussion. My parents would kill me if I didn't go through with the wedding—especially since I was four months pregnant.

In 1971 getting pregnant meant I was asked to leave high school before I was "showing." The father, a boy a year ahead of me, got to stay in school. But not me.

It was traumatic saying good-bye to my teachers, one by one, awkwardly explaining *why*, as if they didn't already know. Of course everyone knew. You were secretly front-page news in the small town of Cuba City if you got pregnant and weren't married.

I remember the first girl who found herself "in trouble" when I was in high school. Her parents sent her away, I'm not sure where, but months later when she returned she wasn't pregnant anymore—and her family still loved her. It seemed to me that her parents must have sent their daughter away because they didn't want her to become the talk of the town any more than she already had. Sending their daughter away for a while felt like a loving thing to do, and when she returned I saw her walking down the street hand in hand with her parents. I was amazed: *How could a girl make such a huge mistake and her parents never stop loving her?*

I still don't know the answer to that question.

My parents never forgave me.

After my daughter was born I went back to finish high school, but not without "a little help from my friends." Frustrated because I couldn't get back into my clothes, a friend assured me, "No problem, try some of these." And she handed me some little white pills. My friend was right. The pounds quickly melted away, and so did the harsh feelings about myself. I was full of energy, finished high school while working part time, and even though my husband and I were young, my speed-induced euphoria convinced me we could make our marriage work, raise our daughter, and live happily ever after. But soon a stack of unpaid bills interrupted the fairy tale and I realized we weren't playing house anymore.

My husband's day job didn't pay enough to make ends meet, so I started working the graveyard shift in a factory. Punched in at 11:00 p.m. and for eight hours stood on a platform, grinding lenses for safety glasses. Eight spools lined up in a row in front of me—put a lens in each spool and take one out—kind of like a juggler spinning plates on top of those skinny poles. It was a mindless job; yet never boring. Because the graveyard shift was really a soap opera—every night a different story line—and considering my *still-wired* condition, I fit right in.

It wasn't unusual for our third-shift manager to offer someone a ride to work, or more truthfully show up at an employee's home and beg them to come to work so he wouldn't have to fire them. Refereeing marital arguments in the break room, hunting down an employee's teenager out carousing in the wee hours, the guy would do anything to make sure production numbers added up in the morning and quotas were met.

Brought up with a strong Protestant work ethic, I certainly did my part to help out. I'd fine-tuned my chemistry by then, so almost every night I met quota two hours before the end of my shift. This was my first grown-up job and from my manager's perspective, I was a shining success. So why did my life still feel so messed up?

Eventually I left the factory job and I left my husband, too. (Mother wasn't right—I didn't learn to love him.) So here I was, a nineteen-year-old single parent not receiving any child support, can't afford child care, it's freezing outside, and the heating-oil tank is empty. I applied for assistance and food stamps. This definitely was *not* a recipe worth keeping, but for a couple more years I kept repeating it anyway, including getting married again.

Of course the second marriage didn't work any better than the first. I'd just turned twenty, and after a few months of wedded bliss discovered my new prince charming was gay—but how could a girl refuse such a romantic proposal?

"Hey, maybe we should get married?"

"Okay, why not," I said, shrugging my shoulders, "it would certainly save money."

As a reader looking in, you must be wondering how this lifestyle affected my daughter. That's what I wish I had been concerned about, too. But I wasn't. I provided for my daughter, but the unfortunate reality is that a child can't raise a child.

Thank heavens, after ending my second marriage, I decided to end another bad habit in my life, too. No big epiphany—the loose wires in my brain didn't suddenly connect, so I made a conscious decision to clean up my life. Addicts don't think rationally. Instead this addict was scared clean. I nearly died a couple of times when I almost overdosed. Finally I had the good sense to send my daughter to stay with my folks, lock myself in my apartment, and not answer the door when certain "friends" knocked. For two weeks I was so sick I prayed for death. Miraculously I stayed clean after those two weeks, but horrible flashbacks haunted me for another year.

Always looking for the positive side in life, the good news about being addicted to drugs was that I qualified for free tuition in a program for recovering addicts at the local technical college. *Okay, so what did I want to be now that I was all grown-up?* Thumbing through the school's catalog, looking at career choices, I decided it might boost my self-confidence if I tried to do something I didn't know anything about. So I enrolled in the two-year auto mechanic program.

It was 1976. I didn't realize it when I signed up, but I was the first woman to ever enroll in the program, which meant I was the only female in a class of twenty-three students. The instructor, a short, stocky, ex–Marine sergeant wearing black-rimmed glasses, navy pants, and a short-sleeved maroon shirt that had his name embroidered above the front pocket, was just what I would have expected.

But I *didn't* expect what happened next. On the first day of class, as soon as the instructor entered the room he headed straight over to my

experienced when I was working for Fern, apparently I'd picked up through osmosis from hanging around the supper club. As a hard worker, day and night, most of my time was spent at The Farm Kitchen. Any free time should have been spent with my daughter, but it wasn't. Instead, every night after work, I'd go out to the bar and "have a few." Fern cleaned me up so I looked like a smart girl, auto mechanics proved I was a smart girl, but when it came to my personal life, I was still a mess. No drugs, but vodka and hideous choices in men were just as lethal.

Why do some women gravitate toward bad boys and downright losers? I'm still not sure, but before I met my husband, Bob (we'll be married thirty-two years this December), that was my M.O. Put me in a room filled with men, thirty of them great guys who treat women with kindness and respect because it comes naturally, and instead of going after one of those gems, somehow I'd lock on to the three losers in the room every single time. Even if a loser wasn't interested in me, I'd keep on trying to get his attention. In fact when a man wasn't interested it made him even more desirable.

Fortunately even hooking up with a loser had its perks. Imagine every morning having someone professionally wash and style your hair, including trimming any split ends, so by the time you walk out the door your hair looks picture-perfect. No doubt about it, Alan was a big-time loser who berated me for living in the low-rent district, and for decorating the walls of my townhouse with cheap art (even though he didn't mind living in my abode rent free), but at least he was a hairdresser (unemployed, of course) and I could talk him into styling my hair every morning before I went to work. (If you dig deep enough you can find something positive in the midst of every loser.)

Losers like Alan the hairdresser had been the only guys I'd ever dated until I was introduced to the man who did the best typesetting for miles around.

One of my first assignments before The Farm Kitchen opened was to get the menu printed. My boss handed me a typed list of entrees with prices and I was supposed to figure out the artwork, choose a paper stock, and find a printer. But I didn't know anything about printing and I'd never even heard the word *typesetting* before, so the first thing I had to do was some research. Unfortunately I ended up doing "just enough" research to drive the man at the quick-print shop crazy.

"I'd like it printed on Beckett Cambric paper. The front of the menu should be a drawing of a barn, with a chicken sitting up in the loft and when the barn doors open, the menu is printed inside. Cool, huh?"

But the man just kept shaking his head. "Listen, lady, I'm a quick printer. You're talking a dye-cut and other stuff that I don't do here."

Nevertheless, I kept right on listing the little "extras" I'd like to add. "If we could? Pretty please?"

Totally frustrated, he finally pointed to a display of books on the counter. "See this book? Read it and then go see Bob Beecher, the guy who wrote it. He owns Setype, a typesetting company here in town. Beecher has patience, I'm sure he'll be happy to explain anything you want to know." Then he shooed me out the door.

The printer was right about the book. Even for a novice like me it was an easy read. But before I got around to going to Setype and meeting the owner, I had what might be described as a setback.

My latest loser boyfriend couldn't style my hair every morning, but he did own a Harley. (A Harley qualified as one of those loser perks I told you about.) When we were out for a sunny afternoon spin, even though the traffic light was shining "green-to-go," which meant we had the right of way, a man driving a convertible made an illegal turn in front of my boyfriend's Harley and we—CRASHED! My makeshift seatbelt (arms clasped tightly around my boyfriend's waist) didn't quite do the trick. Immediately following impact, my body became a human projectile. I flew through the air, landed in the front seat of the convertible, hitting the driver so forcefully that my body caused injury to his, and then I ricocheted off the driver's chest and landed on the other side of the road in the middle of the pavement. Instead of my head, the helmet I had snugly snapped in place split in half. I imagine the "Flying Suzanne" was right up there with one of Evil Knievel's early stunts, but I didn't remember any of it—didn't even remember riding in the ambulance. I was out cold.

When I finally came to in the emergency room two hours later, the only thing I could remember, and it was my biggest concern, was where I worked. "I don't know what my name is, but I do remember where I work," I told the doctor who kept asking if I knew what month it was. "Could someone call, describe what I look like, and tell them I won't be in today?"

My dedication to work has never surprised me. When I was a kid, blood would have to be gushing—in a steady stream—before my mother would let me stay home from school. And when I was feeling sick to my stomach on the first day of fourth grade, Mom insisted it was a case of first day nerves. "Tough it out," she preached. "Hopefully someday you'll have a job and you won't be able to call in sick because of every little ache and pain. So get dressed, you're going to school."

But the pain in my side continued to get worse and I kept insisting I couldn't possibly go to school. Furious, eventually my mother delivered an ultimatum: "If you're too sick to go to school, then I'm taking you to the hospital instead. How would you like me to do that?"

"I wish you would," I begged.

The emergency room intern told my mother if she'd waited thirty minutes more, my appendix would have burst.

When I finally did meet Bob the typesetter for the first time, I still looked pretty banged up from the motorcycle crash—bruises, hobbling on crutches, one leg in a cast, the other completely wrapped in an ace bandage, and I was sipping a vodka tonic to help kill the pain. My doctor's prescription had been three weeks bedrest. But The Farm Kitchen was opening soon and if I wanted to keep my job, I needed to get that menu finished.

Not only did Bob Beecher run Setype from an office in the basement of his townhouse, he also owned *Ad City*, a local Madison weekly shopper. Divorced, but granted full-time custody of his two children, Bob worked from home so that he could spend more time with his son and daughter.

Unlike the quick printer, Bob the typesetter was sympathetic to my *impossible* menu concept. He even complimented me on coming up with the idea, especially since I didn't know anything about printing. But he did agree it wasn't a job for a quick printer: "Not to worry," Bob told me. He'd make sure the menu was finished in time for the restaurant opening.

I was impressed—not only was this guy talented, he owned two businesses, took full-time responsibility for his children—and he was a handsome man. Gorgeous, really, but I could only dream. This responsible clean-cut guy was way out of my league.

"But love is blind, and lovers cannot see," wrote Shakespeare, which must account for Bob's impression of me the first day we met: "I was a single parent, working around the clock trying to run two businesses, couldn't remember the last time I'd had a date, or even left my house except to go to the grocery store—and there you were. A goddess walking into my office asking for help. It was love at first sight. You were a smart girl—I knew it right away—and you were hot!"

Hot? A banged-up woman with a crazy idea for a menu, walking on crutches, one leg in a cast, the other completely bandaged, and drinking a vodka tonic in the middle of the day when she was supposed to be working—just what was it that made me so lovable?

Bob may have thought I was hot! But he was a typical guy—he never called.

I was the one who finally called him three months later, but not about a date. I needed advice—business advice. Bob seemed like a successful businessperson and since I was a customer, I thought he might not mind.

🌀   🌀   🌀

Some people read in the bathroom, but not me. I did commercials. Wedged kitty-corner on the left side of the kitchen near the sink and refrigerator, the one-and-only bathroom in our house must have been an afterthought, because the door, sink, toilet, and tub were squashed so close together when you opened the door, you had to maneuver your body around it to actually get into the bathroom.

You know the phrase "Necessity is the mother of invention"? My mother was too cheap to buy a lock for our bathroom door, so it was a toss-up: Either people out in the kitchen could hear me pitching the "Guaranteed eight-hour fresh scent protection of Secret Roll-On Deodorant," or they'd open the unlocked door (assuming the bathroom was unoccupied) and catch me with my pants down.

So there was only one choice for this kid. Whenever I was sitting on the toilet I'd reach over and rummage through the vanity drawer, pull out a bottle of mouthwash, deodorant, or can of shaving cream, tilt my head to the side—ever so slightly—smile, hold up the product, look into the imaginary camera and (loudly) deliver the advertising copy from the back label using my "commercial voice." Folks in the kitchen, on the other side of the thin bathroom door, smiled and found my commercials quite amusing.

That's the problem with pretending—when you're a kid it's cute, but when you're all grown up, and a housekeeper at a Marriott hotel in Manhattan opens the door when you're not expecting it, things can get a little embarrassing.

I didn't hear her initial knock and the "Housekeeping" shout-out because I was onstage dancing in front of a full-length mirror, my Nano playing with the headset turned up high, a bottle of spring water substituting for a microphone, and in a disco fever I was swinging my hips and singing along out loud with Irene Cara's *Flashdance*.

> *What a feeling, bein's believin',*
> *What a feeling. I can't have it all, now I'm dancin' for my life.*

To this day I'm not certain just how long the housekeeper had stood there watching my performance (another reason to always latch the privacy lock on your hotel room door). But in the middle of my final bow, I realized I had an audience, which might have been only a minor embarrassment (because I'm really a pretty good singer), except I forgot to put the cap back on the water bottle. So as I was gracefully genuflecting, the water ran out of the bottle, down my leg, and puddled on top of the Scotchgarded carpeting. When I looked up the housekeeper was applauding.

Since I wasn't a cute, pretending ten-year-old, what was my explanation? Apparently when you're an adult, you don't need one. I can only imagine what the housekeeper said to her supervisor. "There's a nut-job in room 1412. Clean that room later!"

One of my goals in life is to be approachable. If someone walked into a room filled with strangers, I'd like to be the stranger they felt comfortable enough with to come over and talk to. Don't get the wrong idea. It's not like I'm out to save the world, and I have no desire to solve everyone's problems, but I think it brings people a lot of comfort when they feel like they're not alone. I know it does for me. And that's why I'm not afraid to admit I'm still one of the great pretenders.

I'd just finished giving a speech about "Pretending My Way to Success" to a group of librarians, when a young woman from the audience came up front to speak to me. There were tears in her eyes as she told me how relieved and amazed she felt to hear that I never went to college. "Everyone I work with has graduated from college," she said. "Most have a master's degree, but I've only graduated from high school. I always feel like everyone I work with is smarter and I worry that I'll never fit in."

I smiled and assured the young woman that it wasn't a piece of paper she needed. And then I told her this story. . . .

My husband and I used to live in Madison, Wisconsin. The University of Wisconsin is there and it has a lovely student union terrace that faces out over Lake Mendota. Frequently in the summer, live entertainment was featured on the terrace and my husband would ask if I wanted to go. I loved the idea of spending an evening sitting by the water and listening to music, but every time I went near the university's campus, I started feeling anxious and sick to my stomach.

I never let on how I felt, so my husband and I did go and sit on the terrace a few times and listen to music. But it wasn't ever a pleasant evening for me. I knew he would enjoy it and it had been such a romantic gesture that I didn't want to spoil the evening. But I just couldn't relax. Because when I looked at the people sitting around me, I felt like they were all in a different league.

I didn't have a degree. Instead I spent my college years starting a restaurant and publishing a business magazine. But then one day when a professor from the University of Wisconsin called, asking me to speak to his business class about my magazine, I realized that what I'd been looking for I wasn't going to find in school.

The problem wasn't the piece of paper—the problem was me. It took a long time to find my self-confidence. I always knew it was inside of me. Sometimes I'd come close to spending an afternoon with it, but then someone would say something that seemed to be out of my reach, and I was back to feeling unimportant in the world.

But when the professor called and asked if I would share my business experiences with his class, not only did I give a great lecture, I was finally ready to move on. I "graduated" that day. I told the young woman standing beside me in the library that "today" she'd graduated, too.

My Famous "Almost" Beef with Broccoli

I must have a real knack for pretending, because for twenty-some years I served my Beef with Broccoli recipe to family and friends and no one ever asked, "Where's the beef?" But when I shared the recipe with folks who read my daily column at DearReader.com the emails immediately started pouring in.

"Suzanne, is everything all right? I was reading your Beef with Broccoli recipe in today's column, but there isn't any beef in the recipe. Where's the beef?" So I dug through my recipe file and sure enough I found beef clearly printed at the top of my recipe card *Beef with Broccoli,* but when I read through the recipe, there wasn't any beef—what happened to the beef? And the bigger question, "Where's the beef been all these years?"

Reviewing the recipe I realized that instead of beef, I'd been making the recipe with mushrooms. It's amazing that all those years no one ever asked, "Suzanne, is this Beef with Broccoli, or Mushrooms with Broccoli?" To which I would have replied, "Of course it's Beef with Broccoli. See those mushrooms on your plate? They're a newfangled kind of beef. Vegetarian beef. They came from a cow that had a real thing for mushrooms." So where's the beef? I'm still looking. In the meantime, trust me, this is a fabulous recipe. You can call it what you want, Beef with Broccoli, or "Almost" Beef with Broccoli, and you'll have a fun story to tell at the dinner table.

This recipe serves 6, but I always double it.

1½ pounds broccoli
2 tablespoons cornstarch
2 tablespoons cold water
¼ cup vegetable oil
8 ounces mushrooms, sliced (not too thin)
1 medium onion, sliced thin
2 cloves garlic, crushed or finely chopped
½ teaspoon salt
½ cup chicken broth
2 tablespoons soy sauce

couple of the verses meant. But for some reason I felt at peace—which was something I hadn't experienced for a very long time. I don't know how many times I reread Chapter 7, but eventually I drifted off to sleep.

The strangeness of the night felt even more bizarre in the morning. But it hadn't been a dream, because there was my Bible lying on the floor next to the sofa. I picked it up and started reading Chapter 7 again. Verses 13 and 14 were especially comforting. "Consider the work of God; who can make straight what he has made crooked? In the day of prosperity be joyful, and in the day of adversity consider; God has made the one as well as the other. . . ."

I read the chapter again in the tub when I was getting ready for work, and before I left, I announced to my husband and kids what had happened and I read Chapter 7 aloud. My family was tolerant, yet loving, saying things like "That's great, Mom," and "I'm glad you finally got a good night's sleep, dear."

I took my Bible to the office and went through the entire story again for my secretary. She was tolerant and kind. All right, so no one was as moved as I was about my 2:00 a.m. experience, but that was okay. I needed rescuing, they didn't. And over the next few months I stood on the promises I felt Ecclesiastes Chapter 7 was going to deliver. I thought for sure things would turn around and the magazine would start making money—but nothing changed. The magazine continued to lose money—lots of money—so now I was even more pissed off than before my 2:00 a.m. "experience."

So that's the way it is, huh? The Big Guy comes to my rescue, makes me feel all warm and fuzzy and confident—and for what? More of the same? You've got to be kidding!

Finally, one afternoon, alone in my car, I was yelling, "Just what the heck am I supposed to do here? I've tried everything to make this magazine profitable, I'm juggling money, paying bills on a hope and a prayer, and practically losing my mind. The stress is killing me. I wanted to sell the magazine, but no . . . you made it clear to me that it's not time to sell, that I'm supposed to keep it going. So, Big Talker—do you have any miraculous ideas about how in the hell I'm supposed to make payroll next week?"

No answer.

So I called a meeting for all of the employees from both *In Business* and my husband's typesetting business and explained the dire situation. "We've got to work together to try to solve this problem or we're going to go under." I realized there really wasn't anything more that staff could do to make the magazine profitable. Everyone was working hard. But at least the meeting alleviated a huge amount of stress, because I didn't have to pretend things were okay anymore.

The magazine's financial situation continued to worsen. Sometimes I felt it was rebelling, actually fighting back, because everything I tried to do to cut costs backfired. Printing the monthly magazine was the biggest expense, so I decided to get bids to see if I could find a better price. Line by line, I went through each company's bid comparing it to what I was currently paying, and finally I found a printer who promised to cut my printing bill by $2,000 a month. But after I made the switch to the new printer, my first bill came in $850 more than I used to pay.

How could things go from bad to worse? There wasn't much fight left in me. I pretty much gave up and took the attitude, whatever happens, happens. Two weeks later (eight months from my middle-of-the-night "experience"), I knew in my heart it was time to sell. In my eyes nothing had changed. The magazine wasn't financially any better off than it had been eight months ago, but there was no doubt in my mind, and the Big Guy was giving his stamp of approval—it was time to find a buyer. But how do you sell a magazine that's not making any money?

My CPA assured me people buy companies for all sorts of reasons that have nothing to do with money. A potential buyer would think with their expertise, they'd be able to turn the magazine around and make it profitable. Hearing the CPA's encouraging comments was a bit of a double-edged sword: *Step right up! Be my guest! If you think you can make this magazine profitable, if you think you can do a better job than me, I'd like to see you try. . . . I've poured my heart and soul into this thing . . . it won't hurt my feelings one little bit!*

But please, somebody buy this magazine.

My CPA's instructions were to focus only on the basics. "Show prospective buyers what the magazine grosses before expenses. They can figure out what their costs will be based on the suppliers they decide to use."

In other words, I didn't really have to come right out and say the magazine wasn't profitable. But it didn't seem logical, because the type of businessperson who could pay the huge asking price wasn't going to be an idiot. They'd quickly do the math. And I was right. It didn't take long for interested buyers to figure out the magazine wasn't a break-even venture.

"Yet it only takes one," my savvy CPA reminded me, and she was right. People do indeed buy businesses for all sorts of reasons other than money. The man who ended up buying *In Business* wanted instant recognition in the local business community, and instant recognition was one thing the magazine could indeed deliver.

There's an old saying in the boating industry: "The two best days of owning a boat is the day you buy it and the day you sell it." I'd have to agree those were the two best days of owning a magazine, too. When my husband and I launched *In Business*, it was truly an exciting day, and the day I sold *In Business* for over a quarter of a million dollars—enough to pay off the debt I'd accumulated, and to write a check to the government for its share of my huge windfall, with money left over to buy a house and furnish it from top to bottom—was also a glorious day.

But still it was a melancholy sale. I needed to sell, clearly it was time to let the magazine go and I felt relieved, but it also felt like I was saying good-bye to a friend, and even worse, I left feeling like a failure. In spite of the money I made at the very end, the magazine hadn't been successful. But ironically, success was the topic a businesswomen's group asked me to talk about at one of their upcoming meetings.

I didn't think about it when I agreed to do the speech, but as I was preparing my notes all I could think about was here we go again. The magazine was still misleading people, giving the impression I was rich and successful, when I wasn't. Why did I agree to give a speech about success? This was stupid. What was I going to say to these women?

I began to cry and once again the Lord came to my rescue.

"Suzanne, it makes me feel so sad to see you crying. I'm sorry you don't feel the magazine was successful, because in my eyes, it was a huge success. It did exactly what I needed it to do."

I've never quite figured out what the real agenda for *In Business* was, but I do know if publishing the magazine hadn't been such a stressful time in my life, I probably wouldn't have ever started Meals for Madison, a non-profit free meal program.

Eight of the eleven years I published the magazine, Meals for Madison was my emotional savior. It was the perfect business. (Dare I say a match made in heaven?) I was passionate about the work, there were absolutely no cash-flow worries, and at least 125 customers were lined up every Friday noon waiting patiently for me to open the door. I loved to cook and most of all, I absolutely loved to wait on people—still do. I'd rather be a server at a party than one of the guests. (Though I do admit I love having a reason to buy one of those cute little dresses that makes me think, *I'd look fabulous in that, but where would I wear it?*)

The director of the Neighborhood House Community Center (the oldest community center in Madison, Wisconsin), on South Mills Street, wanted to start serving free noon meals. It wasn't like I had a lot of extra time on my hands, but it felt like there should be something more to life than trying to make the magazine profitable, so I went to an informational meeting.

Representatives from several different local organizations were at the meeting. I've never been a group kind of person (maybe because I was an only child and I'm used to doing things by myself), so when the director announced he was looking for groups to sponsor noon meals, I raised my hand. "Put *me* down for the second Friday of every month."

But when the director asked what group I represented and I told him "Just me," he reiterated what was involved in serving a meal: Cooking, money, people, time, it was a big commitment. How did I plan on pulling it off by myself? I assured him I'd buy the food, do all of the cooking at home in my big sunny kitchen, call friends and ask them to help me serve. If need be, instead of working at the office, I'd have some of my employees help serve the meal. "Don't worry about it. I will absolutely take care of everything one Friday noon a month."

Two months later my initial once-a-month commitment had turned into creating my own nonprofit organization, Meals for Madison, and I started serving a noon meal every single Friday. Friends gladly volunteered to help, but when my employees helped serve one of the meals, seeing how much they enjoyed the experience gave me a new idea. I started offering the Meals for Madison volunteer opportunity to other companies, and soon there was a waiting list.

Sponsoring a meal involved making a cash donation to the program, usually $250, and sending eight to ten employees to help serve the meal. A cross section of the company would show up, from the president on down. I think people were so excited about the opportunity to give, because they could actually see where their money was going and they could get directly involved, without a long-term commitment.

Folks like to roll up their sleeves; there's nothing worse than showing up to volunteer and finding there aren't enough jobs to keep people busy. My volunteers got a real workout—setting up tables and chairs; covering tables with paper tablecloths, salt and pepper shakers, plates, glasses, and silverware; making coffee; organizing the buffet table; driving to pick up catered food donations from restaurants; and making deviled eggs—for most volunteers it was their first time. Oh, they'd eaten quite a few deviled eggs, but they'd never made them before. I grew up on deviled eggs, and to this day whenever I serve a big meal, deviled eggs are on the table in Grandma Hale's deviled egg dish.

The day before our free meal I'd hard-boiled 11 dozen eggs. Three volunteers would be responsible for peeling and cutting the eggs in half, mixing up the filling, thinly slicing green olives for garnish, and then topping off the filled eggs with a light sprinkle of paprika or dill weed. Corporate executives in suits and ties were smiling and giggling like little kids after they finished filling 264 deviled eggs.

One of the jobs for two volunteers was to make the "weekly Friday run." Local restaurant owners like Jim Delancy, one of my biggest supporters, encouraged me to call for a donation every week if needed. Jim would have his chef prepare the main course, another restaurant owner donated tossed salad and dressing for 125 guests, Schoeps Ice Cream company set aside three 5-gallon tubs of ice cream for pickup every Friday, bakeries made fresh dinner rolls (and sent day-old bread for our guests to take home), a paper company donated the plates, cups, silverware, and napkins, and the local dairy donated individual cartons of white and chocolate milk.

Every month I reserved a full page in *In Business* for photos of volunteers and a list of thank-yous to companies who helped sponsor a meal. No one ever refused a request. Whatever I needed for Meals for Madison suddenly appeared. I never ran short of money to buy things like huge Nesco warming pans, coffee pots, and other serving items for the program. I worked very hard, but I had a lot of fun, too. *Why couldn't it have been that way with* In Business *magazine?*

Eventually I got high-school students involved. During the school year, on the fourth Friday of the month, ten high-school students volunteered at

something was terribly wrong. I'd never seen such a runny deviled egg filling. It had the consistency of soup. We reviewed the instructions. Yes, he mixed mayonnaise and yellow mustard (to taste) just as I'd instructed, so why was the filling so thin? But then I looked down in the wastebasket and there were twelve egg yolks. In my list of ingredients I'd forgotten to mention egg yolks, so he'd tossed those out in the trash.

I was repeating the instructions I'd heard my Grandma Hale tell me for years. Grandma never wrote her recipe down. "Suzanne, just mix a little mayo and mustard together." And that's exactly what my cooking student did.

Grandma made deviled eggs by "feel." When the filling felt right, it was time to fill the eggs. It's still how I make deviled eggs today, but I'll give you some approximate amounts to start with. There are all kinds of fancy recipe fillings for deviled eggs, but my family loves this simple approach.

12 hard-boiled eggs, cut in half
Mayonnaise
Yellow mustard
Pepper

Scoop the yolks out of the eggs and mash them with a fork. Add 3 heaping tablespoons of mayonnaise, 3 long squirts of yellow mustard, and 2 dashes of pepper.

Mix well, then wash your hands and stick your finger in the mixture. Taste it to determine what it needs—more mayonnaise or mustard, or both. The mixture should be creamy and taste good to you. Wash your hands again, mix some more, and do the finger test again, until it tastes right.

Using a teaspoon, fill each egg. Slice green olives with pimentos and stick one vertically in each egg. Lightly sprinkle paprika on top of some eggs, and dill weed on others.

6. The Boogeyman Just Might Be Under My Bed!

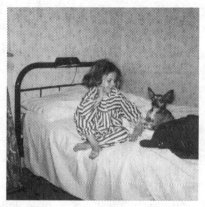

Grandma and Grandpa Hale grew popcorn, so once a year the entire guest bedroom floor would be covered with rows and rows of popcorn cobs drying on top of newspapers, which was pretty exciting for a kid, except at night when I had to tip-toe through the popcorn to get to the bathroom.

Fear comes over me a lot easier than it used to. Maybe it's becase I've been around for a while, been down too many roads, know too much, and experienced too many things—had my mother die in my arms. It changes you.

I never used to give things a second thought. If I got an idea and thought it was worth pursuing, I did. There wasn't any consideration for how it would change my life or that I might not succeed. It might not have been the best approach to take, but it was my style and I was comfortable with it. But lately my style has changed. I seem to be more cautious. Looking in from the outside, you'd think a more cautious attitude might bring me a sense of security—but it hasn't. Instead it's made me more uncomfortable with myself and taken away a lot of my joy.

My husband and I go for a walk every day and as we're strolling through the neighborhood, it's not unusual for us to start brainstorming about new ideas. Back and forth, his idea, my idea—we've done it for years. It's always been "play" for us. But the other day when my husband started talking about a new business idea, I noticed that listening to him was making me uncomfortable—actually quite irritated. I could hardly wait for him to pause so I could blurt out a list of reasons why his idea was dumb and we certainly didn't want to do it. But that's not the way we've always played the brainstorming game. So what was up with me? And in the midst of trying to figure out why I wasn't willing to entertain new ideas, even just for fun, I realized that fear was the problem.

Okay, so what exactly was I afraid of, and why was this fear showing up all of a sudden? I wasn't sure. Maybe I was afraid to entertain any new ideas just in case one of them became a reality. But that never used to stop me; sorting and sifting through different ways of looking at things, it's always been part of the joy in my life.

Thankfully, sometimes recognizing I'm afraid of something, even if I can't figure out *why*, is enough to conquer the fear, and that's what happened this time. When my husband and I went for our morning walk the following day, we both enjoyed playing the brainstorming game again.

I don't know about you, but the boogeyman does in fact hang out underneath my bed, especially at three in the morning. One of my favorite books suggests you should feel the fear and do it anyway, and I'd have to say that's usually the choice I make. But when fear strikes and I'm in the middle of a big "showdown," I'm hyperventilating, curled up in the fetal position, and clinging to my pillow while desperately trying to talk myself out of an anxiety attack.

The problem with fear, at least my kind of fear, is that it's difficult to label. Most of the time there isn't a rational explanation for it. Most of the time my fear is all wrapped up in a lack of self-confidence. People think *I can*, I've told them *I can*, but I'm afraid *I can't. Oh no, what have I done? What was I thinking? If I can't make this happen, I'll be ruined.* Lack of self-confidence has always been my boogeyman and probably always will be.

My first inclination is to joke about my lack of self-confidence and put a lighthearted twist on it. A friend even chided me when I mentioned I was going to write about it. "Talking about a lack of self-esteem—it's old news, Suzanne—been written to death and no one wants to read about it anymore."

I felt hurt. Here I was telling the truth, putting my lack of self-confidence out there for him to see and what does he do? Tells me it's unimportant, I'm being a big baby, and it would be embarrassing to write about such a thing.

Well, I'm here to tell you (and him) the subject is alive and well in my life. Questioning my abilities, talking myself out of feeling like a loser, these are conversations I know by heart—both sides. The boogeyman doesn't even have to actually say anything to taunt me, I do that job myself. *Suzanne, you're not talented, you're a big loser, people think you're strange, crowds of people are snickering behind your back, every other writer is in, but you're out.* The list could go on for hours and, unfortunately, some days it does, until even I have had enough—*for heaven's sake, Suzanne, give it a rest.* I get upset and angry with myself—and that's when the "magic" happens. Because in my weakness I find my strength. Get me angry and I come out fighting. Not fisticuffs, but with just enough feistiness to protect my feelings and in the process, I decide *I'll show 'em I can accomplish great things,* and so I do.

Sun Tzu, in *The Art of War,* said, "If you know the enemy and know yourself you need not fear the results of a hundred battles."

Years ago I decided that if I was going to spend so much time worrying and fearing the worst, I might as well use the boogeyman's visits to my advantage. So I got to know the enemy and here's what I discovered.

Sometimes fear is simply a holding pattern. I know what I need to do, I really want to do it, but I'm still trying to muster up the courage. So even though I feel afraid, I remind myself nothing bad is going to happen, I'm simply circling the airport and killing time, until the clouds clear and it feels safe to land. When I finally decide I can deal with the consequences of my decision—no matter how things turn out—the fear subsides.

Eleven years ago I found myself in one of those holding patterns when I was trying to find the courage to write a letter to my parents. My folks and I never had a loving relationship. Truth is, they never really liked me all that much, and when I got pregnant at sixteen—that was it for them. Embarrassed and ashamed, they couldn't ever bring themselves to forgive me. Even when I was an adult, raising my own children, my father continued to joke about my getting pregnant in high school.

I guess I watched too many episodes of *Leave It to Beaver* because I never gave up on the idea of having a meaningful and caring relationship with my parents. We were all adults now, why couldn't we at least be good friends? It took three years to find the courage to write the letter to my folks and then it took another six months before I found the courage to mail it. When I finally decided to mail the letter, I felt pretty calm and confident about my decision, until I got to the post office and was standing in front of the mailbox. Then reality set in and I fell apart.

Shaking and trying but failing not to cry in public, I stood in front of the mailbox, staring at it—for a very long time. When I finally pulled back the handle so I could drop the letter in the box, I couldn't let go of it. I couldn't release my grip. *Oh my God, if I send this letter, my parents will probably never talk to me again.* But I also couldn't go on with the way things were. Eventually I let go. Sending that letter was the beginning of a new relationship with my parents (even though they quit speaking to me after they read it) because I had conquered my fear.

Fear is one of my loudest emotions. It's one of the best ways to get my attention, sometimes the only way. *Tap, tap, tap, stay with this idea, Suzanne, don't let go of it, even though it seems crazy and makes you feel uncomfortable.*

I'd spent the afternoon at the beach reading the book *Girls in Trouble* by Caroline Leavitt. It's a story about Sara, a sixteen-year-old who's pregnant and decides to give her baby up for adoption. Reading the book was dredging up some pretty powerful emotions that I hadn't felt in a long time. I wanted to stay at the beach and finish the book, but it was getting late, so I packed up and headed home. But I couldn't get Sara out of my mind. I pulled the car over to the side of the road, grabbed the book, and started reading. Pretty soon I was crying and the next thing I knew I had an overwhelming need to call the author.

I didn't really know Caroline Leavitt. We'd been introduced through a friend of a friend and that's why she'd sent me a copy of *Girls in Trouble*. But her phone number was printed on the bottom of the note card she'd tucked inside the book, and the next thing I knew my fingers were dialing and the line was ringing on the other end. Voice mail picked up and after the beep, in between some pretty loud sobbing, I left an emotional message about how I was pregnant at sixteen, how I could relate to Sara's feelings, and that until I'd started reading her book, I didn't realize all of this was still tucked away inside of me. But then immediately after I said good-bye and hung up the phone, fear consumed me.

Are you nuts, Suzanne? What is this woman going to think? You don't even really know her and you leave a crying, blubbering message about how you can relate to Sara, a fictional character in her book. Panicked and embarrassed. The edgy nervous fear that prompted me to call the author in the first place had turned on me. Now it was a scary *You're going to look like a fool* kind of terror.

But thankfully, in the midst of fear, most of the time there's something good waiting for me. Thirty minutes later when Caroline Leavitt phoned

Whistle While You Work

My toilet whistles at me. It's kind of a sly little "Yoo-hoo! Come hither!" sort of whistle. This is a new thing for me and my toilet. Our past propinquity has been the customary toilet/owner relationship. We keep each other clean and tidy.

Don't get me wrong—I applaud creativity. So at first, a whistling toilet was actually quite amusing. I was even a little boastful, thinking I probably had the most entertaining toilet on the block. Why, my toilet whistles every time I flush! It even puckers up in the middle of the night for no apparent reason. But now this whistling thing is beginning to get a little irritating.

You know how a joke is hilarious the first time out, still funny the second go-around, but after three times, the punch line just doesn't do it for you anymore? Well, my toilet has whistled one too many tunes.

I asked friends if they had any ideas about how to solve the whistling toilet mystery, but they were only amused. "Why does your toilet whistle, Suzanne? Maybe it wants to play 'Name That Tune'? Maybe it thinks you have a cute butt."

Okay, it's time to call a professional.

"Joe's Plumbing. Can I help you? . . . Why does your toilet whistle? . . . Well, maybe it thinks you've got a cute—"

Yeah, yeah, I've heard that one before.

Suzanne's Whoops! Banana Bread

When I was young I spent a lot of time in Grandma Hale's kitchen. Every now and then I'd hear her say, "Hmm, I guess I'm in-a-pickle," which meant Grandma just realized she goofed when she was mixing up a recipe and it was too late to go back and fix her mistake.

Frequently I find myself in-a-pickle when I'm cooking, too. The phone rang and then a FedEx delivery showed up at my door. Even though I'd made my banana bread recipe a hundred times before—"Whoops!"—I put way too much buttermilk and a little too much baking powder in the batter, but there was no turning back now. So I popped the banana bread into the oven. And guess what? I ended up with the best-tasting banana bread I'd ever made. Of course, then the challenge was to try and figure out exactly what I did wrong. After a couple of trial-and-error attempts, I did, and here is the incredibly tasty result. . . . It keeps great in the refrigerator, too!

Makes one loaf

1¼ cups mashed very ripe bananas (the riper or browner the bananas are, the better the bread will taste)

2½ cups all-purpose flour

1¼ cups buttermilk

½ cup granulated sugar

½ cup packed brown sugar

¼ cup vegetable shortening

2 eggs

3 teaspoons baking powder

1 teaspoon salt

½ teaspoon baking soda

½ cup (overflowing) chopped walnuts

½ cup chocolate chips

Preheat oven to 350 degrees. Grease bottom only of either a 9 x 5 x 3-inch loaf pan or four small mini pans. Beat all ingredients together, scraping bowl, just until blended. Pour into pan(s). Say "Whoops!" before you pop it in the oven and 50 to 60 minutes later, if you're baking one loaf, or 35 minutes for four smaller loaves, you'll be biting into a tasty, moist slice of banana bread.

Be sure to bake until a wooden toothpick comes out clean when inserted in the center. Immediately remove the bread from the pans after you take them out of the oven. And you really should cool the bread on a wire rack before you slice into it, but that never happens at my house.

out of leftover wood from a church that Amy's relatives helped build when she was a little girl. It was the cross Amy and I used every Tuesday when we said communion together and it sits on my fireplace mantle today.

I don't know what other folks were thinking about at Amy's funeral, but I could hear her playing the piano in the swing band, I felt the hug she gave me the first day I knocked on her door, and when it came time in her funeral service to say Amen, I asked the Lord to please take good care of Amy, the woman who taught me that life is more interesting when you have the courage to roll a *not-so-perfect* piecrust.

🌸 🌸

Pie Boy

Rolling a piecrust. It's an old-fashioned art that will impress your friends. Even though we're surrounded by high-tech gadgets, it's amazing what a simple wooden rolling pin can create. Take a homemade pie to a family dinner—announce that you rolled the crust from scratch—and your relatives will *ooh* and *ahh*. It's a real self-esteem boost, even for a twelve-year-old boy.

Years ago when I was homeschooling my son, I also taught a cooking class twice a week to eight other homeschooled kids. Our first lesson was how to mix and roll a piecrust. The holidays were just around the corner, so I thought it would be fun if the kids could impress their families by making pies from scratch. Mix and roll the dough, toss out the dough because "oops, somebody goofed," mix up another batch, and finally roll out the finished piecrusts. We cut miniature leaves out of the leftover dough, painted them using food coloring, and circled the edges of our cherry, apple, and pumpkin pies with an assortment of fall leaves.

The kids enjoyed making pies, especially one twelve-year-old boy who got so hooked that he started baking pies every night at home. "We've never seen him so interested in something." His parents sounded a bit bewildered. I think they found their son's interest in baking pies a bit odd, but I was overjoyed. So I didn't mind one little bit when Pie Boy, as I lovingly refer to him now (because over the years I've forgotten his name), called me one evening at ten o'clock. When the phone rang I was in the final stages of tucking myself into bed, just getting ready to pull the covers up, position my pillow, and drift off.

Ring, ring. "Mrs. Beecher, I'm sorry to bother you this late at night. My parents said it was too late to call, but I told them you wouldn't mind. I just finished making two pies, using the recipe from class, but I put peaches in instead of apples. What temperature would I bake them at and for how long?"

Pie Boy had taken it upon himself to experiment, imagine that! I'd never seen a kid have so much fun baking pies. He baked so many pies that by the time we finished our class six weeks later, that boy was a better pie maker than me.

Over the years, I've lost track of my amazing Pie Boy. I wonder what he's doing today. Is he a professional baker? Or maybe he's a Wall Street broker and every year he amazes the relatives on holidays and at family reunions as they watch him make pies from scratch, rolling the dough and even cutting fancy leaf borders. I'm sure his pie-baking skills might have even impressed a date or two along the way. "Hey, how about baking some apple pies tonight?" What woman wouldn't be impressed?

"Where did you ever learn how to bake pies?" someone might ask. And wouldn't it be a magical moment if he told them about the woman who taught a cooking class when he was homeschooled. Who could have imagined . . . a pie-making lesson from Amy, to me, to my Pie Boy.

Amy's Piecrust

This recipe makes one crust. You'll need to double it, or mix it up twice for a two-crust pie. Don't worry, Amy will be cheerleading for your success every step of the way.

    1 cup sifted all-purpose flour
    ½ teaspoon salt
    ¼ cup cold lard or solid shortening
    2 to 4 tablespoons ice-cold water

Mix flour and salt together. Cut lard into the flour mixture until crumbs are about the size of small peas. Add cold water, a little at a time, mixing with a fork until the dough just holds together. Amy always emphasized using only enough water to hold everything together. Roll out the dough. Line your pie tin. Fill, crimp edges, and bake at the temperature your pie recipe recommends.

Never Fail Piecrust

This recipe makes five crusts. The name says it all; you just can't fail when you're making this piecrust. If you're a beginner, this is the recipe for you.

    4 cups all-purpose flour, lightly spooned into a cup
    2 teaspoons salt
    ½ cup water
    1 tablespoon sugar
    1¾ cups shortening (not lard or butter)
    1 egg
    1 tablespoon apple cider vinegar

Mix all ingredients well and divide into 5 balls. Slightly flatten each like a giant hamburger, cover with plastic wrap, and refrigerate until cold if using right away. Or you can freeze for later use. (To freeze, wrap each one in wax paper and freeze in a freezer bag—you'll always have a piecrust on hand. This dough won't get tough if you re-roll it.)

9. Bull-Puckey, I Can Do This

On the way home from visiting my parents one Easter, I spotted a herd of cows (I love cows) so my husband pulled the car over. It's hard to feel sexy when you're wearing dark wraparound glasses and using a red-and-white cane, but these cows seemed to know I needed a support group. They gathered around and my husband took this photo.

If anyone had told me when I was first diagnosed with benign essential blepharospasm that eventually I wouldn't mind having an eye disorder, in fact I'd even wrap my arms around it with love, I would have felt mightily insulted.

How dare they suggest some Pollyanna make lemonade out of lemons bull-puckey crap? (Bull-puckey. In lieu of cursing, it was one of Grandma Hale's colorful words.) But the reality is that after a period of grieving, I did fall head-over-heels in love with my eye disorder and we're still good buddies today. Don't get me wrong, I'd be in line tomorrow for a cure, but in the meantime I feel like one of the fortunate ones. Because learning to love your disorder, that kind of magic doesn't happen for everyone.

10. Please, Give This Woman a Job!

All dressed up for a job interview, but a little too young to get a work permit.

Once my eye disorder and I called a truce we quickly adapted to each other's wants and needs and settled into a routine. I even started working again, from an office in my home, helping out in my husband's new software company, the Computer Group. Working from home was the perfect place for benign essential blepharospasm and me to get along. I could take a break whenever I needed, and because bright lights caused painful headaches behind my eyes, my husband installed dimmers on all of our light switches. Boy, did it ever feel good to be able to work again. I'd never realized how much of *me* was wrapped up in my job until I couldn't do it anymore.

Some people dream of the day they'll finally retire, but not me. I plan to keep on working right up until my final breath, then take a few vacation days to see who shows up for my funeral, after that get used to my new surroundings (hopefully ocean-front, maintenance-free property), and then I'll be ready to go back to work.

One of my biggest fears about death is I'm afraid I'll be bored. Bored stiff, so to speak! (Couldn't resist!) I know, I know, the sales pitch is strong—satisfaction guaranteed. The streets are paved with gold, you get an automatic face-lift and tummy tuck when you pass through the Pearly Gates, you don't have to share a room, the water's nice and hot the minute you turn on the tap, and you get to see all of your friends and loved ones who have passed on before you. My Grandma Hale and I have made a date for brunch the morning after I check in. Worry is a thing of the past and there's no need to work.

See, it's that last perk—*there's no need to work*—that concerns me.

I like to work, I love to work, and it's satisfying. To me it's playtime. I've seen only a couple of episodes of *Touched by an Angel*, the show where angels were given assignments here on earth, but the idea appeals to me. I'm looking forward to an afterlife career. I'm multitalented, look good in white, and I'm not afraid to fly. I only hope I'm heavenly material. (Since you're reading my book, may I use you as a reference when the time comes?)

My eye disorder and I had become so adept at working together at home that I began wondering: If I didn't tell someone there was something wrong with me, would they even know? And the more important question: Could I function in the real world? What a scary thought. But I needed to find out, so I searched the classified ads looking for a part-time job. It had been fourteen years since I'd had to look for a job, so it felt strange putting together a résumé and trying to figure out what I wanted to do. But then again, maybe the job title wasn't all that important. After all, the real reason I wanted to work outside of my home was to see if I could.

WANTED: PART-TIME VOLUNTEER COORDINATOR FOR NURSING HOME . . .

Compared to publishing *In Business* magazine and running the meal program, I guess most people would have thought that a part-time volunteer coordinator at Sunny Hill Nursing Home was a nothing sort of job. But I wanted this job more than any job I'd ever applied for, or thought about applying for, in my life. This job could be my test and it sounded like fun, too.

When I handed Sunny Hill's activity director a copy of my résumé, she immediately tossed it aside. "I don't need to look at this," she said. "I know you used to publish *In Business* magazine and recently sold it. To be honest, I really called you in for an interview more out of curiosity than anything else. Would you please explain to me why you're interested in this part-time hourly wage job?"

Nothing on the outside suggested my real motives. I intentionally hadn't worn my dark glasses, even though I knew the fluorescent office lighting would cause horrific pain in my eyes, and I'd taken a Valium before the interview so my eyelids wouldn't be blinking nonstop. Stress caused my disorder to be in full bloom and I figured if the activity director knew I was disabled, then I wouldn't get the job. If she didn't ask, I wasn't going to tell. (Okay, so she *sort of* did ask, but I had a second truth waiting in the wings just in case the question came up.)

"Yes, it's true I am plenty qualified for the job," I agreed, "maybe even a little overqualified, but now that I've sold the magazine, I'd like to work part time at something I'm interested in—you know, keep myself busy with something that's fun. And I think setting up a volunteer program for your nursing home would be fun."

My reasons sounded logical and the activity director said the job was mine if I wanted it. But she felt too embarrassed to tell me what the hourly rate was. "Would you give me a few minutes while I speak with the nursing home director about giving you a raise?"

I liked this job already. A raise before I even started! Word must have gotten around that I was a professional widget assembler, too.

My first day at Sunny Hill was routine: filling out forms, learning how to properly punch in and out, studying the rules and regulations book and then signing off that I understood everything I'd read, and finally a tour of the facility. Now that the boring stuff was out of the way, where was I supposed to hang my hat?

Since volunteer coordinator was a brand-new position at Sunny Hill there wasn't any "old" office to occupy, so I'd be sharing. Fine with me. I wasn't expecting anything fancy, which was a good thing, because after the activity director ushered me into my new office, she handed me a vacuum cleaner. "See that stuff over there in the corner? If you push it aside, you should be able to squeeze your desk in there. Go ahead and vacuum the carpet while you're waiting for the maintenance guy to bring a desk up from storage."

The office and desk weren't important. Just give me a phone and some heat! It was freezing in that office! I mean the kind of cold where you leave your coat and gloves on, wear two pairs of socks, and curl your feet up underneath your butt so you can warm them up while you're sitting in your chair. Apparently my new office always had a heating problem—in that it had no heat at all—because there weren't any heating vents in the room. The "office" used to be an elaborate storage closet. The lack of heat didn't bother my new roommate, because she never spent any time in the office. First thing in the morning she'd drop her coat and papers on her desk and then spend the rest of her day on the floor, interacting with residents. It was way too early in my employment to complain, so I made the best of the situation and bundled up.

Okay, so I had a desk, the floor was vacuumed, my paperwork all filled out nice and neat. Now what exactly did a volunteer coordinator do? My job title suggested (pretty definitively, if you ask me) that I'd be coordinating volunteers, but since there weren't any volunteers at Sunny Hill, I assumed the first thing I needed to do was recruit some. But the hows and whys of the job left a lot of room for interpretation, so I asked the activity

my folks decided we were going to Expo 67, the World's Fair in Montreal, Canada. I guess I was too young, or too shocked to ask, "Why are we going to the World's Fair?" That vacation is still a mystery to me, because my dad never went anywhere unless there was free beer or old people.

"Aged Advice" gave residents a chance to switch roles with staff. Instead of residents asking for help, suddenly staff needed help from the residents. Employees weren't shy about asking questions, some so personal they were submitted anonymously.

"Our son wants to dye his hair orange! What should we do?" Ninety-five-year-old Alice's advice: *"In the grand scheme of things, orange hair isn't a big deal. Your son will grow out of it and if he goes anywhere with you, just make him wear a hat."*

"My husband says I pay more attention to our dog than I do to him. I don't agree, but my husband's getting pretty upset about it lately. Don't you think he's being silly?" —Mother of a precious Pekingese

I thought this question called for a man's Aged Advice, so I asked Edward, who'd been happily married twice, but had outlived both of his wives.

"I don't know if I can help you, but here we go . . . I wasn't ever too good at guessing, so I liked it when my wife told me what she needed. What did she want for her birthday and should I get the blue one or the pink one? I could buy something extra, but I wanted to make sure I made her happy. Both of my wives were kind and loving women and my best friend. A dog can be man's best friend, but you've got a husband who is telling you he wants to be first in your life and then the two of you can love that precious Pekingese together."

Still single at ninety years old, Margaret offered unbiased advice for this Sunny Hill employee's yearly family dilemma.

"Dear Aged Advice, every Christmas we make the rounds, visiting my parents and my husband's parents. This year I want to stay home with my husband and our two children. My husband disagrees and thinks we should go visit our

parents. What do you think?" —*Hoping to have a home-cooked meal at my house this year*

Dear Hoping, my advice is to find your recipe box and start cooking. Get out some paper right now and send an invitation to the relatives. Invite them to your house this year. Tell them they deserve a break and just to seal the deal, throw in that it's your way of thanking them for cooking all those years. My mama said I should always graciously accept a thank-you. I hope this helps."

"Aged Advice" received local television and newspaper coverage and the corporation who owned Sunny Hill presented the facility with an award, too. I was thrilled that Sunny Hill got press and was recognized by Corporate, but I was even more excited to see employees grabbing a copy of the monthly newsletter the minute I put a stack in the lobby. Eventually my "press run" grew large enough that I was able to sell a few ads to local businesses to help cover production costs.

Since I was making up my own job agenda as I went along, I added a weekly cookie-baking class to my part-time schedule. When I first thought about baking cookies with the nursing home residents, visions of Grandma Hale's kitchen danced merrily in my head. Bowls, measuring spoons, mixers—I had all of the ingredients lined up on kitchen tables for the first day of class. How exciting! Line by line, I'd read the recipe while residents measured and added the ingredients to their own mixing bowls and pretty soon we'd be eating warm-in-your-tummy homemade chocolate-chip cookies, just like Grandma used to bake. But baking with elderly folks in a nursing home who are there because they need a high level of care—what was I thinking? I quickly realized this would never be like Grandma Hale's kitchen.

Ten people sitting around the table, each at a different skill level—what a challenge it was to give everyone the assistance they needed! While I was helping Abby measure one teaspoon of vanilla, Bert opened the package of flour and dumped it on the floor. Eighty-nine-year-old Sarah could use the measuring spoons, but couldn't read the small print—does that say ½ or ¾? Sandy grew impatient with all of us and started eating the chocolate chips right out of the bag. Lillian probably could have mixed up one hundred cookies without any assistance and quickly lost her patience waiting for everyone else to catch up. And then there was Fred, who just wasn't up to doing anything. He needed complete one-on-one assistance. I describe these folks with love. They were each doing the best they could, and I was the one who needed to rethink things and make a change. The purpose of this class wasn't about taking me back to baking in Grandma Hale's kitchen. Instead I wanted to create a "Grandma Hale" memory for each of the residents.

So I asked family members to bring in one of their mom's or dad's favorite cookie recipes, and in addition to baking and eating some mighty good cookies, we'd get to hear a story. "Sarah, can you remember when you used to bake these cookies?"

Baking class started at nine-thirty on Wednesday morning and about an hour later, nursing home employees would just happen to be walking by the kitchen to see if we needed a taste-tester. After a few weeks, the residents and I started getting requests. "What kind of cookies are you baking next week? Can I buy some to take home?"

Soon my baking buddies and I were in the cookie-baking business. Old favorites like peanut butter, snickerdoodles, chocolate chip, and oatmeal raisin were top sellers, but our real moneymaker was the apple-cutout sugar cookies. Selling the cookies at cost meant the baking supplies didn't have to come out of my budget.

I'd been working at Sunny Hill for almost a year, when I realized the job had become routine. Routine in that context meant success. My eye disorder hadn't improved, but I'd learned how to compensate and work around it. I'd passed the test. Yes, indeed, I could successfully work a job outside my home and make a go of it in the real world.

Having been "the boss" most of my life, I realized what a hassle and time-consuming job it was when an employee gave notice: running an ad, interviewing, hiring, training, and waiting for the "newbie" to actually be able to earn their keep. So I gave my boss three months' notice, hoping she'd be able to make a smooth transition. And I let her know if she found someone before three months time, I'd be happy to leave early.

At first she ignored my resignation, which was kind of flattering. When I'd ask about placing an ad or helping to train my replacement, she'd smile. "You're not really leaving, are you? Tomorrow, we'll talk about it tomorrow."

But finally, two months later during one of our familiar walk-and-talks, my boss accepted the idea that I'd really be leaving Sunny Hill. Sad to see me go, she sent me off with not one, but two going-away parties and two serving bowls that I still have today. But the best going-away gift Sunny Hill gave me was the option of continuing my health insurance for eighteen months. I didn't realize it until the eighteen months ran out, but when it did, no company would insure me because of my preexisting condition— good 'ol benign essential blepharospasm.

My husband and I started working together again, but his small group policy had limitations, and my preexisting condition was one of them. The only way I could possibly get health insurance again was if I could get into a large insurance pool, which meant going to work for a big company. I needed health insurance, but my husband and I loved working together and had really missed that closeness during the year I worked at Sunny Hill.

So my little crazy brain went into overdrive and I came up with two possible solutions that would allow me to get health insurance and still continue to work with my husband: get a divorce, become an Avon Lady or a Mary Kay Representative.

"Absolutely not! You're out of your mind!" My husband wouldn't even let me finish explaining why we should get a divorce. But I wasn't kidding. What if something happened to my health? Without insurance I'd drain our savings and we'd both be destitute. This way, if we got divorced, the State would have to provide medical assistance if anything terrible happened to me. I was willing to pay for health insurance, but since no company would sell me a policy . . . the look in my husband's eye suggested the discussion was closed, so on to Plan B.

"Ding, dong, Avon calling."

Every two weeks the Avon Lady stopped by our house when I was a kid. My mother was cheaper than cheap, but every other week she placed an order, which she hid from my dad: bubble bath, lotions, lipstick, eye shadow, wrinkle cream—and the Avon Lady gave free samples, too. My favorites were the little miniature lipsticks in the white tubes. Come to think of it, those miniature lipsticks are probably why I'm so hooked on the miniature shampoos and lotions the fancy hotels give away—blame it on the Avon Lady.

Avon offered health insurance. I wasn't sure about all the details, but I also was afraid to ask right away, because I knew my name had been added to the insurance blacklist pool. (Insurance companies shared their rejection information with one another.) So I decided to become an Avon Lady first and ask questions later. Maybe I could slide into their group insurance pool without being detected. And as backup, just in case Avon rejected me, I became an official Mary Kay representative, too.

I wasn't planning on ringing doorbells and actually trying to sell Avon or Mary Kay products. Instead, my plan was to buy all the products myself. I'd purchase the minimum amount a representative was required to sell, and then eventually when I'd worked for them long enough, I'd try to get in their insurance pool. (Ironically the only makeup I ever used was lipstick, so my friends were well supplied with cosmetics for a few months.) Unfortunately, both brilliant insurance schemes failed. Nobody wanted me and my preexisting condition.

A few months later, none of that mattered because my husband and I decided to move to Florida. What a surprise it was when I discovered that in addition to palm trees and warm ocean breezes, the state of Florida required insurance companies to cover preexisting conditions, even in a small group policy like the one my husband had for his business.

Hallelujah! I finally had health insurance again!

Apple Cutout Sugar Cookies

1½ cups confectioners' sugar
1 cup butter or margarine, softened
1 egg
1½ teaspoons vanilla extract
2¼ cups all-purpose flour
1 teaspoon baking soda
1 teaspoon cream of tartar

Frosting

2 cups confectioners' sugar
¼ cup light corn syrup
2 tablespoons water
Red and green food coloring

In a large mixing bowl, combine the first seven ingredients in order given and mix well. Chill dough for 2 to 3 hours or until easy to handle. Roll out on a lightly floured surface to ¼-inch thickness. Cut with an apple-shaped cookie cutter dipped in flour. Place on greased baking sheets. Bake at 375 degrees for 7 to 8 minutes or until lightly browned. Cool on wire racks.

For frosting, combine sugar, corn syrup, and water in a small bowl. Transfer three-fourths of the frosting into another bowl; add red food coloring for apples. Add green food coloring to remaining frosting for stems. Frost cookies. Allow to sit overnight for frosting to harden.

11. He Loves Me, He Loves Me a Lot

My husband, Bob, and I are best friends and still crazy in love, even after thirty-two years.
Photo by John Allaman.

My husband says he was put here on earth to take care of me. Now how could a woman possibly argue with that kind of logic?

Our marriage must be for keeps because every day it just keeps getting better and better, even after being married for thirty-two years and working together every single day. But working together harmoniously wasn't something that came about naturally. Shortly after we were married, we went several times to see a therapist so we could learn how to work together. "Learning" required *several* sessions because it took me a while to recognize and to finally 'fess up to the fact that I tend to think my way of doing things is the right way. (And just between you and me—most of the time it is! I'm smiling, just kidding.)

Seriously, my husband and I learned a lot about each other in those "shrink" sessions, and over the years, we've developed a Recipe for our Marriage. . . .

My husband gives me a foot rub every night, I bake chocolate cakes from
    scratch—they're his favorite.

I wash and dry, he folds and puts away.

He takes care of the trash, I do the gardening.

He kills any misplaced bugs, I leave the room while he's hunting them down.

He encourages me in whatever new thing I want to try, I reciprocate.

And when I ask, "Honey, do I look fat in these pants?" my husband reassures
    me I don't. "The older you get, the sexier you look, dear."

We're both committed to making our marriage work, but more impor-
tantly, my husband and I are best friends. We enjoy being downright silly
and strange sometimes, like when we lived in Wisconsin and we used to eat
lunch in the hospital cafeteria.

The hospital's food tasted great, I'm not kidding. And the price was
right, too, especially when I was wearing a black suit, because the cashier
would automatically assume I was a doctor and she'd give my husband and
me the employee discount. The first couple of times we thought it was a
fluke, and didn't even realize we'd been given a discount until later, when
we were looking at our receipt. So to test our "black suit" hypothesis, we
conducted our own clothing-discount experiment and after pitting pastel-
colored suits up against black suits, we did indeed discover that our theory
was correct. Only my black suit was discount worthy. When I wore pastel
we paid full price.

Most people would shake their heads and wonder, *Why would anyone
want to eat in the hospital cafeteria?* But those lunches are delightful, funny
memories for my husband and me—a wonderful recipe from our life.

Yes, my husband and I are best friends, but unfortunately he never
gets very excited about extending our circle of friends. Every time I suggest the idea of getting to know our neighbors—"How about inviting
some people over for dinner?"—he changes the subject. So it was a real

of Payless Shoes, but we looked even more out of place later that evening, when we ended up dining at Wendy's.

That year's anniversary plan was to keep the evening spontaneous, so we hadn't made a dinner reservation. But by the time we'd cruised around town and spent time window-shopping at the mall, it was eight-thirty, we were starved, and every restaurant we stopped at had a long waiting list—except Wendy's!

So what the heck—"Table for two, please!" And we dined on two singles with cheese, two fries, and we even ordered ice cream Frosties—after all, it was our anniversary!

"He loves me, he loves me a lot!"

Cooking with My Husband— Our Favorite Recipes

It was a long Labor Day weekend, so I challenged my husband to a Bread Bake-Off Contest. The only rule was that the bread recipes we used had to include yeast. My husband found a Hearty Wheat Bread recipe on the back of a package of gourmet flour. And I decided to make two entries: a Northern Maine Oatmeal Bread (a recipe I'd never tried before) and a Daisy Braid from an old, reliable, sweet dough recipe.

One of the first steps in my husband's Hearty Wheat Bread recipe instructed him to warm up the mixing bowl, so of course he got out the hair dryer, turned it on full blast, and aimed it at the inside of the bowl (everyone interprets a recipe a little differently). Okay, I admit it worked. The hair dryer did warm up the bowl, but maybe he should have used the low setting on the dryer, because his bread didn't rise—at all. Yeast can be tricky. If the water you add is too hot, it kills the yeast, and if it's too cold, nothing happens.

After the first bite of my Oatmeal Bread and Daisy Braid rolls, my husband awarded me the Bread Bake-Off Blue Ribbon and suggested it would be better if I didn't even taste-test his bread. The poor guy's Hearty Wheat Bread turned out so hearty that in his words, "If we ever decide to build that addition to our house, we can make the bricks out of this dough."

Northern Maine Oatmeal Bread

Years ago I found this recipe in an old cookbook. It looked good, but I never tried it until our Bread Bake-Off Contest. I couldn't get the loaves to rise as high as they should have, but the bread was still fantastic. Next time I'm going to put the pans on top of my dryer to rise, cover them with a dish towel, and then turn the dryer on high. (Another dryer tip from my husband, but this one actually works.)

Makes 2 loaves

2 cups boiling water
1 tablespoon butter
1 cup rolled oats
1 package active dry yeast
½ cup warm water (110 degrees)
½ cup molasses
2 teaspoons salt
5 to 6 cups all-purpose flour
Melted butter

Combine boiling water, butter, and rolled oats in a bowl and let stand for one hour (or 30 minutes if you're using "quick" oats).

Dissolve yeast in warm water. Add yeast mixture, molasses, salt, and as much flour as you can stir into oat mixture. Mix thoroughly. (I use my KitchenAid counter mixer on low.)

On a lightly floured surface knead dough for 6 to 8 minutes, adding more flour if necessary to form moderately stiff dough. (I use the dough hook on my mixer to knead the dough.)

Place dough in a greased bowl and turn the dough over once to grease the surface. Cover with a damp cloth and let rise in a warm place until doubled in size, about 45 minutes. If it's a warm, sunny day put your bread pans in the car. The dough will rise and your car will smell like freshly baked bread. Or do some laundry and set your pans on top of the dryer while you're drying clothes.

Punch dough down. Divide dough in half. Cover and let rest for 10 minutes.

Shape each portion into a loaf and place in a greased loaf bread pan, seam side down, and let rise again until almost doubled in size, 30 to 40 minutes.

Preheat oven to 375 degrees. Bake for 30 to 40 minutes or until bread tests done. (I tap the top of my bread—if it makes a hollow sound, it's done.) Remove loaves from the pans and brush the tops with melted butter to soften the crusts. Cool on wire racks.

Hot 'n' Sour Soup

Hot 'n' Sour Soup, an easy recipe, is my husband's favorite. Even though I'd been making it for him ever since we were married, I never actually tried the soup myself until a couple of years ago when Bill, a friend from Oregon, came to visit. Bill's favorite soup is also Hot 'n' Sour, so to look polite at the table, I ate some of my own creation. It was delicious! All those years I was afraid to try this strange-looking soup. Now I double this recipe because it keeps great all week long in the refrigerator.

Serves 6

3 dried wood ears or 4 dried mushrooms
20 dried lily buds, optional
1 boneless, skinless chicken breast half
1 tablespoon dry cooking sherry
4 cups chicken broth
½ cup sliced bamboo shoots (half an 8-ounce can), drained and cut into
    matchstick pieces
4 ounces bean curd, drained and cut into ½-inch cubes

3 tablespoons distilled white vinegar
1 tablespoon soy sauce
½ teaspoon ground white pepper
2 tablespoons cornstarch
3 tablespoons water
1 egg, lightly beaten
1 teaspoon sesame oil
2 green onions, cut into 1½-inch slivers

Place wood ears and lily buds (if using) in separate bowls. Cover with hot water. Let stand for 30 minutes. Drain and squeeze out excess water. Pinch out hard knobs from center of wood ears and discard. Cut wood ears into thin strips. (If using mushrooms, cut off and discard stems; cut caps into thin slices.) Cut off and discard hard tips from lily buds.

Cut chicken crosswise into thin slices; sprinkle with sherry. Let stand for 15 minutes.

Bring chicken broth to a boil in 3-quart saucepan. Add wood ears, lily buds, chicken, and bamboo shoots. Reduce heat and simmer, uncovered, for 3 minutes. Add bean curd, vinegar, soy sauce, and white pepper. Cook for 3 minutes more.

Blend cornstarch and water in a small cup; stir into soup. Cook, stirring, until slightly thickened. Turn off heat. Stirring constantly, slowly pour egg into soup. Stir in sesame oil and onions.

Potstickers

On my thirtieth birthday my husband planned a surprise birthday party for me. Not only was I totally surprised, he even managed to have me unknowingly do all the cooking—except for baking the birthday cake. Every other week a girlfriend and I were in a routine of cooking together for fun, and my husband overheard us making plans to cook several Chinese dishes the next time we got together. Our next cooking date just happened to be May 25th, the day before my birthday.

"Surprise Birthday Party" May 25th, at 6:30 p.m. The menu was all of the Chinese dishes my girlfriend and I had made earlier in the day, including Potstickers and Braised Shrimp with Vegetables.

Braised Shrimp with Vegetables

Makes 4 servings (I always double this recipe.)

1 tablespoon vegetable oil
1 pound raw medium to large shrimp, shelled
8 ounces fresh broccoli, cut into small pieces
8 ounces mushrooms, sliced (not too thin) or canned whole button
    mushrooms
1 can (8 ounces) thinly sliced bamboo shoots
½ cup chicken broth
1 teaspoon cornstarch
1 teaspoon oyster sauce
¼ teaspoon sugar
½ teaspoon minced fresh ginger
⅛ teaspoon pepper

Heat oil in wok or large skillet over high heat. Add shrimp and stir-fry until shrimp turns pink. Add broccoli and stir-fry for one minute. Add mushrooms and bamboo shoots and stir-fry one minute more. Combine remaining ingredients in small bowl and mix. Pour over shrimp and vegetable mixture. Cook and stir until sauce boils and thickens.

12. Somebody Should Have Told Me About This!

My son and daughter-in-law filled my lawn with pink flamingos one year for my birthday. I loved them so much that after the rental company came to take them away, I bought two dozen pink flamingos of my own.

Up until the moment my husband and I landed at the small St. Petersburg, Florida, airport, this Wisconsin girl had kept pretty close to home. But now the Florida sun was shining on my face, a light warm breeze was blowing through my hair, and palm tree branches were swaying high up in the sky just like in the movies—surely I must be in heaven.

I realize that my moment in the sun may sound somewhat insignificant, but keep in mind that my husband and I had never traveled anywhere warm when it was freezing cold in Wisconsin.

"SOMEBODY SHOULD HAVE TOLD ME ABOUT THIS!" I shouted, arms raised high over my head, hands waving frantically in the air as I descended the ramp onto the tarmac. No doubt every passenger on board heard my proclamation, but I didn't care. Truly I was amazed! Earlier that morning snowplows had been working hard to clear the six feet of snow that had accumulated overnight in Madison, and because I didn't want to have to lug my winter coat along, I practically froze to death running from the airport parking garage to the terminal. But four hours later, here I was in a little bit of paradise.

The only reason my husband and I had even thought about vacationing in Florida was because friends of ours had recently moved and they extended an invitation: "Come on down, it's eighty degrees in January," and they insisted we stay at their house.

I didn't need to do anything fancy on our Florida vacation—just waking up to the warm sun every morning was vacation enough for me. After three days in paradise, I suggested to my husband that next winter we should vacation in Florida again—only instead of two weeks, "Let's make it three, dear." Two days later I was pitching four weeks, three days after that five weeks sounded reasonable to me, and by the time we were ready to head back home, no doubt about it, next year's winter visit shouldn't be anything less than two months. Then again, on second thought, what the heck, let's just move to Florida and visit Wisconsin in the summer.

Initially, my husband's enthusiasm about the idea of moving to Florida lagged way behind mine, until I mentioned the word *boat*, and then the tipping point came quickly. In fact, by the time our plane landed in Madison, my husband had tipped so far over, he pictured us living on a 52-foot Irwin sailboat. "We could rent an office for our business and live on a boat in a fancy marina. The big marinas have laundry facilities, stores within walking distance, cable television, bathrooms, showers, and even a pool!"

Yeah, boy, what more could a girl want? It wasn't exactly the picture I'd had in mind when I mentioned the benefit of year-round boating in Florida. But then again, I do think it's every man's dream to own a boat. Owning a boat is a grown-up boy's version of a tree house, only on the water. Fix it up, tinker a bit. Invite your friends over to trim the sails, cleat the jib sheet, and just hang out, because as "real" boaters know, you can accomplish all of these things without ever leaving the dock—and most boaters never do.

I was hoping my husband wouldn't, but he finally popped the question. "Suzanne, could you imagine living on a boat for a year? How about it?"

Well, I was speechless. After all, it's not every day a girl gets an invitation to live on a boat (thank heavens). How would I fit all of my clothes in those little, itty-bitty boat compartments? And where would I put my treadmill? My husband had that *won't-you-please-pretty-please* look in his eyes, I just couldn't say no—but I emphasized it would be only for one year. So on our flight back home, excited yet nervous, we drew a line down the middle of a piece of paper and wrote down the pros and cons of moving to Florida. What did we have to lose?

Wisconsin's fall season (my favorite time of year) had practically become nonexistent, winters were freezing cold, and weren't we still shoveling snow last Easter? Our software company was virtual and since all of our employees worked from their homes, it really didn't matter where our business was located. If we didn't like living in sunny Florida we could always move back to Wisconsin.

So ten months later my husband and I packed up a U-Haul truck and headed south on I-90. The entire first year after our big move, this girl was on a Florida high, but thankfully *not* on the high seas. In the process of buying our 52-foot Irwin "home," negotiations fell apart. The seller pulled some strange last-minute maneuvers, which made my husband so disgusted with the entire transaction that he passed on buying the sailboat. Instead, we rented a house on the water near the marina. Lucky me, to this day I get brownie points for agreeing to live on a boat for a year, even though I never actually had to do the deed. (It's a great story and whenever my husband tells it, he beams with pride in front of the other men in the room!)

We may not have ended up living on a boat, but my husband did go a little boat crazy. The marina became our second home and guess what card we never left home without?

Sea Tow!

Sea Tow is a "road assistance" type card for boaters. You pay $95 a year, and if your boat breaks down, or if you run out of gas, Sea Tow will come to your rescue—no charge. It was a real deal for us, because the first few years we were in Florida, Sea Tow had to come to our assistance so many times I thought my husband and I would be their first customers to ever be refused a renewal membership. At the very least, I expected Sea Tow to add a "Bob and Suzanne Beecher–only" clause, stipulating that we were required to give them advance warning before we left the dock so they could have a Sea Tow boat and crew on standby.

Our Sea Tow adventures all started when my husband bought a new-used boat and the man who sold it to him failed to mention the faulty gas gauge. The selling-a-used-boat code of ethics seems to be, "If they don't ask, then don't tell 'em." And of course my husband never inquired, because he'd already fallen in love with the boat, sight unseen. He'd fallen head over heels the very first day he read the classified ad—even slept with it under his pillow that night. Nope, he didn't feel comfortable asking too many questions when we finally got our first look at the boat, because in my husband's eyes "she" was already a member of the family.

Wood rot, leaky motor, mildew, these were just some of the problems I noticed, but my husband assured me they were all minor repairs. How could we possibly turn our back on little *Solitude?* (Yes, he'd already named our new arrival.) So we trailered our little bundle of joy home.

A couple of weeks later, when we left the dock on our maiden voyage, I noticed *Solitude*'s gas gauge read half-full. Later in the day, even though we'd been cruising on the water all afternoon, the gas tank was still at the half-full mark. But when I voiced my concerns to my husband he started bragging about how great the gas mileage was in his new boat. Minutes later, we heard the sputtering sound of an engine desperately trying to suck up its last few drops of life from the gas tank. That was our first—but certainly not our last—call to Sea Tow.

My husband replaced the gas gauge, but *Solitude* continued to be a rebellious child, breaking down each and every single time we went out on the water. And, of course, each and every time we had to call Sea Tow. Neither my husband nor I wanted to be the one to make the call. It had become very embarrassing, because by now the guys at Sea Tow recognized our voices.

After a few years my husband finally gave up the ship—literally. But it's hard to break old habits.

What's the card I never leave home without?

Sea Tow! Just in case!

Marinated Flank Steak
A Recipe to Make While You're Waiting for Sea Tow

Our boat had a handy grill attached to a railing on deck. My favorite recipe to make was Marinated Flank Steak. Marinate it at home the night before and simply throw it on the grill. It's fabulous! And if you save a helping for the guys at Sea Tow, they give you a discount (at least that's been my experience).

Flank steak, any size
1 teaspoon tenderizer
Your favorite seasoned mustard (I use Grey Poupon)
3 tablespoons Worcestershire sauce

Score meat crisscross on both sides. Do not cut all the way through. Sprinkle approximately ½ teaspoon tenderizer on both sides of steak. Lightly and evenly cover each side of meat with your favorite mustard. Place meat in a shallow pan and pour 3 tablespoons Worcestershire sauce over it. Turn the meat, cover with plastic, and put it in the refrigerator overnight (8 to 10 hours), turning occasionally. Grill each side for 6 to 8 minutes. Slice thinly and enjoy!

13. Muffins and Mayhem

The two people who brought love into my life when I was growing up, Grandpa and Grandma Hale—and that's me in the middle.

"Warm and sunny, warm and sunny." It's a Florida meteorologist's mantra (in between an occasional hurricane). So it was easy to adjust to the weather when my husband and I moved from Madison, Wisconsin, to Sarasota, Florida. We bid farewell to the snow and cold, but that also meant saying good-bye to cold-weather treasures like tulips and daffodils. They're my favorite spring flowers.

Tulips and daffodils won't bloom in Florida because there's no resting period for the bulbs. Nevertheless, they show up in my yard every spring, because when I was young I learned a gardening secret from my Grandma Hale.

Even though the ground was still covered with a light dusting of snow, Grandma Hale always had the first spring flowers blooming in her yard—because she cheated. Just like seat-fillers at the Oscars, Grandma would carefully line up artificial but realistic-looking tulips and daffodils along the front of her house, until the real "stars" appeared. No one ever doubted that the flowers were real, because Grandma had such a green-thumb reputation.

But it wasn't just the flowers that were a real eye-opener when I first moved to Florida. The animals were pretty strange, too—especially since they tend to show up in places you wouldn't expect to see them. An alligator taking a dip in my neighbor's swimming pool, lizards scurrying back and forth across the sidewalk when I'm out for a relaxing walk, invisible biting flies—appropriately called no-see-ums—and twice a year it's mating season for love bugs. Thousands of females emerge from their larvae looking for an acceptable male suitor and when they find one, they latch on to each other in midair, but instead of rolling over and going to sleep afterward, the two lovers fall to the ground in the heat of passion. Frequently they fall into the path of a moving vehicle. Splat, splat. (What a price to pay for love.) My windshield, everybody else's windshield, and sometimes the entire front end of every single car in Sarasota is covered with a sticky adhesive-like love-bug mess. Superglue should be so strong. And the worst part is, if the aftermath doesn't get cleaned off immediately, the love-bug leftovers will eat right through the paint on your car.

And then there are the roaches. When I moved to the south I was prepared to see an occasional roach—on the floor—but the first time a three-and-a-half-inch cockroach flew across the room (Palmetto cockroaches do indeed fly) and landed on top of the cookbook I was reading, I seriously considered moving back to a cold-weather climate.

Palmetto bugs flying through the air, little black bugs tunneling through my flour—oh, did I forget to mention flour weevils? Well, let me tell you: "Buy-one-get-one-free" isn't really a sale in Florida if it's for flour or cereal—not unless you're going to use a lot of it soon—real soon. I never had a pantry pest problem when I lived in Wisconsin, but if wheat products sit around in Florida for too long—even if they're in a Ziploc bag or a plastic container sealed tightly with a lid—little itty-bitty black bugs hitchhike their way in and set up shop. Bran flakes with raisins seem to be one of their favorites, at least at my house. I suppose even bugs have heard about the benefits of eating bran and staying "regular."

Bran flakes are a staple in my husband's diet, too. He eats about four bowls a day and he doesn't like the idea of sharing his bran flakes with insects. So our solution was to buy smaller quantities and it worked—at least for a few months. But guess who showed up the other day?

I was in the middle of making my Dolly Madison Muffins, had already measured the sugar, eggs, cinnamon, flour, and buttermilk, and had stirred in the rest of the ingredients—including the bran flake cereal. A couple of final swirls with the spoon and the batter would be finished, and that's when I saw it—a bug—scurrying along the counter beside my mixing bowl. Oh no! There was another one, and another one, and when I looked down to survey the situation, there were bugs crawling up out of my muffin batter. Gross!

The bugs were frantic—running for their lives. It was a flour weevil 911 alert! The black critters were panicked, desperately trying to scale the inside wall of my mixing bowl, stopping periodically to shake the muffin batter off their legs—that buttermilk is sticky stuff.

But the batter was like quicksand. The weevils were putting up an organized fight, linking their little legs together like a safety chain, from deep in the middle of the bowl. Some of them had even broken out the emergency landing equipment, their nose plugs and swim caps keeping them dry, while they backstroked to safety. Surely I was in the middle of a horror novel.

Before the batter went into the trash, I must admit a couple of other options did run through my frazzled mind: The little critters are going to get baked at 400 degrees and don't people regularly eat bugs on reality television shows?

I may be a northern transplant, but I think I'm starting to think like a real Floridian. When I told my born-and-raised-in-Florida neighbor my gruesome little black-bug story, he smiled and shared this recipe for "How to Tell When You've Become a Real Floridian"—and it appears that I'm almost there.

> Bugs in your flour?
> A first-year northern transplant throws the flour out with the bath water,
>   so to speak—anything and everything that's touched the flour goes in
>   the trash.
> The second year—where are the tweezers?
> Third year—little black bugs—hey, they're protein!
> Bon appétit!

Actually most Florida critters and bugs are manageable once you learn how to avoid or head off their visits. And there's always a funny story behind the first time you meet up with them. Here are some of my favorites.

Run-ins with Critters from my Recipe File

Knock, Knock. Who's There?

I was flying back home and was in the middle of the most interesting conversation I've ever had at 28,000 feet in the air, or anywhere for that matter.

The woman sitting next to me was a faithful daughter, about my age, who told me that every year right before summer officially begins in Florida, she battens down the hatches on her eighty-year-old father's waterfront condo. The first year the loving daughter did the deed, everything looked secure, so she closed the door and they headed back to Indianapolis. But when she brought her dad back in the fall, it was apparent that someone had sublet their condo without permission.

"It was all new to me," the woman sitting next to me on the plane said, "but since you live in Florida, you probably know all about sewer rats, don't you?"

No, couldn't say that I'd ever had the privilege of meeting one, but I had the feeling I was going to hear all about them. Apparently sewer rats aren't content with their underground décor. And why should they be, when in the summer there are perfectly good Florida condos going to waste? So they pack their bags and move in.

"Knock, knock."

"Who's there?"

It's a sewer rat knocking on your toilet seat.

Yep, rats swim up through the sewer pipes, lift the lid on your toilet seat, walk right into your vacant condo, and make themselves at home for the summer—first one out gets dibs on the master bedroom!

Sewer rats are no fools. While most of us are spending the six weeks before summer trying to get into shape so we look good in our swimsuits, sewer rats are working out with a personal trainer, building up their biceps for the big push—on your toilet seat.

Actually, when you think about it, sewer rats are performing a kind of public service. No need to pay a house sitter to watch your place over the summer, sewer rats will gladly house-sit your condo for free.

Heck, they'll even water your plants if you leave your cable TV hooked up. And a little suggestion: It would be a nice gesture if you left some cheese as a thank-you gift. Everybody likes to be appreciated—even sewer rats.

"But I fixed those sewer rats good the second year," my seatmate continued. "I researched the problem on the Internet. You fill up your toilet with antifreeze, strap duct tape around the rim of your toilet seat, and then top it off with something heavy like bricks."

I could see it now—a kind of hot fudge sundae challenge for the rat. If a sewer rat can hold his breath long enough to swim through the antifreeze, rip through the duct tape with those razor-sharp incisors, and heave-ho, push that lid open, it's paradise for the summer.

And I'd have to say if a sewer rat could make it through all that, I think he's earned his keep, don't you?

Squirrel Psychology

I used to think the little skinny Florida squirrels in my yard were cute. But now we're at war. I didn't start it. Okay, I'm sure if you asked them they'd put the blame on me—but you know how squirrels are.

Last week when I was planting flowers and mulching in my garden, there was a squirrel that seemed to be keeping a pretty careful eye on me. Every time I'd put my spade into the ground, he started squeaking and jumping up and down on the tree limb above me. He was more than persistent, so I assumed he'd buried his food stash in my garden, and I was making him nervous.

I didn't think anything more about it until I sat down to take a break and something hit me hard on the top of my head. When I looked up, I saw the squirrel had found a partner in crime, and they each pitched another acorn at me. Amused, but rubbing the top of my head because those acorns smart, I asked the squirrels nicely to stop. They didn't. In fact, they kept running through the maze of tree limbs, following me around the yard all day long, and they wouldn't quit throwing stuff at me.

I was no longer amused.

I could understand the need for a squirrel to be concerned about his winter food supply, but these squirrels are Floridians. Yeah, yeah, it's been passed down through the generations to store up food for the winter months and these squirrels could be Wisconsin transplants, like me, and they just can't help themselves, blah, blah, blah. My husband has explained all the possibilities to me, but he's sympathetic to those warriors only because they haven't thrown a single thing at him. As far as I'm concerned those squirrels need therapy.

I checked the yellow pages, but there seems to be a shortage of Squirrel Psychoanalysts, so I decided to try my own brand of squirrel psychology. Just how complicated could a squirrel's mind be?

My plan was to convince those yeahoots that there wasn't a shortage of nuts, and then we could call a truce. So before I went to bed, I set a pan of assorted in-the-shell nuts underneath the tree. The next morning the pan was empty. Even so, I have the feeling I'm not going to prevail in this conflict, because when I was walking back toward my house, one of those squirrels *whacked* me with my own peace offering.

Even Mama Snake Needs a Night Out

I don't mind sharing my space with wild Floridian creatures, because I real-ize they're probably thinking *they're* the ones who are tolerating *me*. But the big black snake—the *bigger around than a garden hose* snake—the one that's been hanging around my house lately, we need to come to some sort of an agreement, because he's scaring the bejeebers out of me.

As far as I know, black snakes are harmless. (Usually I love to hear from readers, but if you know something to the contrary, please don't write and tell me I'm wrong—I think I'd rather be in the dark about what this snake likes to eat.)

Black snakes, at least the one that likes to sun himself on my porch, are docile. Mine doesn't rattle and he doesn't rise up and hiss at me. We haven't discussed it, but I get the impression that I make him just as nervous as he makes me. There's plenty of sun to go around in Florida, so I don't under-stand why all of a sudden this snake wants to sunbathe on my back porch.

Let me tell you, once you nearly step on a snake, everything that moves seems to slither. But after a couple of days with no snake on the steps, I forgot about him—until today, when I went out the back door, and my foot landed right beside his head. There we were, side by side on the same step, then he side-winded off, insulted that I'd almost tromped on him—and I was screaming.

There's always a reason for everything, and since I've seen some little baby black snakes around lately, maybe this is really a mother snake in desperate need of a few minutes away from her demanding children.

Maybe she's searching for a day at the spa—a little sun and a little snake cocktail, topped off with one of those fancy paper umbrellas.

Maybe I need to be more tolerant and understanding. I've raised children, heaven knows I can relate.

Slither On up to the Bar

I was planting geraniums in front of my house the other day, feeling all calm and relaxed, when it started to drizzle and the drizzle turned into a pretty good rain. But I kept on working anyway until all of a sudden, in the middle of the downpour, I was surrounded—they were everywhere. Snails! Slimy, disgusting, huge—I'm talking Texas-sized snails crawling all over the very plants I'd just been lovingly tending to.

I've never been squeamish about garden creatures before. Bugs, grubs, they've never bothered me. Big, fat night crawlers—no fear—I bait my own hook and I even talk to them when I'm gardening. "Keep up the good work, guys. Thanks for hanging out in my dirt."

But apparently I've met my match, because when I saw an army of snails crawling all over my geraniums, I freaked! No exaggeration. *What to do, what to do?* I picked a bunch of snails off the geraniums, but when I saw them crawling on my gardening glove, my primal instincts took over. I SCREAMED and flung them into the street. The people in the cars passing by thought I was a nut. "What is this woman throwing at us?" But I couldn't help myself.

"Help!"

I threw my gardening gloves on the ground and went running into the house, yelling for my husband. "You've got to come out and get rid of these snails!"

The snail affront ended my gardening for the day, and the day after that, and the day after that. I was worried I'd never be able to garden again, so I decided to find out how to get rid of snails.

Every relevant website I visited on the Internet had a photo of a snail, but I couldn't even stand to look at one, so I started visiting websites for children. "Meet Mr. Snail!" Yeah, Mr. Snail is supposed to look like a cute little cartoon character, with his smiley face and his little wiggly tentacles, but I knew the truth. Those smiley little slithering things would invade your garden and hunt you down.

Unfortunately I discovered that the best way to get rid of snails is to pick them off the plants, put them in a sealed bag and, well you know. . . . But since I'd already attempted that method and failed, I decided to get the snails drunk. Yes, option number two for exterminating snails is to sink a jar into the ground so the rim is flush with the dirt, fill the jar almost to the top with beer, and watch those snails conga line right up to the bar, fall in, and party to the end.

It's been a couple of weeks since I've seen any snails. My all-you-can-drink beer party was a big hit, but when I walked by my neighbor's house the other day I noticed they'd added a new yard ornament—a ceramic snail. I know it's supposed to be cute, but I still don't like it.

So I think tonight I'm going to have to get it drunk.

The All-You-Can-Drink Lunch Buffet

I'm trying my best to get my work done today, but welts—actually big pink mosquito bites—are bubbling up, especially around my ankles, and it's really getting difficult to concentrate on anything except this itching.

It's driving me crazy. I can't stand it and I shouldn't be itching, because I followed the rules. Life isn't fair.

I preplanned and sprayed myself with a bottle of advanced insect repellent before I went outside to pot some flowers. So instead of my body parts smelling like a lunch buffet—two legs, two ankles, an arm, and even a big toe—the mosquitoes should've been pinching their noses in disgust. "Phew, that woman stinks."

Yes, when that hungry swarm of skeeters buzzed near me they should have been repulsed, because the spray is supposed to trick them into thinking that my blood bank is tainted. Maybe I need to get a refund, because they seem to love the stuff. I swear I saw a swarm of six mosquitoes flying around with straws in their mouths. The little buggers congregated, battle plans were formed, and I heard a loud, humming war chant right before they attacked. I'm so tasty, they even came back for seconds—good to the last drop.

Again, I stress that life isn't fair, because I didn't buy the cheap stuff. I bought the top of the line: "Guaranteed to repel mosquitoes, chiggers, biting flies, no-see-ums, gnats and fleas." But apparently these mosquitoes, now filled with my fresh red blood, don't read labels.

Then again, apparently I don't either. My husband handed me a tube of hydrocortisone cream. "Put a layer of this on and the itching will stop." So I followed his advice, layered it on my arms and was spreading it real thick on my legs, topping off my big toe, when my husband ran back into the room. "Wait! Stop! I gave you the wrong tube. That's the special toothpaste the dentist gave me last week."

So I'm still itching, but at least I smell minty-fresh and my legs are tartar free.

Dolly Madison Muffins

Mix together in a large bowl:

4 eggs, beaten
2½ cups sugar
1 cup vegetable oil
1 tablespoon cinnamon
5 teaspoons baking soda

Then add these two ingredients alternately:

5 cups all-purpose flour
1 quart buttermilk

Next add 6 cups raisin bran (the cheapest is okay).

Mix well by hand. Cover, and let the batter stand in the refrigerator for at least 24 hours before baking.

Fill liners in a cupcake pan with batter. Bake for 20 minutes in a preheated 400-degree oven. (Sometimes I add fresh blueberries right before baking.)

Batter keeps four weeks in refrigerator with or without the little black bugs! Use the batter as you need it. Make three or four muffins every morning.

14. May I Please Have This Dance?

My husband and I dressed in our rented 50s attire, ready to rock at the big dance.

Me, myself, and I. We can be a bit strange sometimes. A good friend called the other day and we made a date for dinner, but ever since then part of me has been trying to come up with reasons why I should call her back and cancel. It's a very weird thing. Whenever I accept an invitation, initially my adrenaline gets a little push and it feels good thinking about doing something fun and different. There's no doubt I'll have a great time. I'm looking forward to the date, and even enjoying thinking about what I'll wear. But the closer it gets to the day of the event, the more uncertain I feel, and that uncertainty continues right up to the time I'm getting dressed to leave. Even then I'm wishing more than ever that I hadn't accepted the invitation. "Why did I say I'd do this? I wish I could just put on my pajamas and stay home."

Moan and groan—regrets about accepting the invitation overwhelm me. But by then it's too late to cancel and it's a good thing, too. Because as soon as I meet my friend and we sit down to dinner my feelings change. And that's when the mystery gets even more bizarre, because in the middle of our dinner it'll dawn on me how much fun I'm having and I'll be chastising myself: *Suzanne, you really ought to get out and do this more often.*

Me, myself, and I. Yes, we can be a strange bunch. Thank heavens people overlook our little bit of strangeness and invite us out anyway. And thank heavens we accept their invitations, or I would have missed two "recipes" in my life that turned out to be unexpected, precious moments.

The first was an invitation from one of the biggest advertising agency executives in town: "Live Band—Dress in 50s Attire." My husband and I moseyed on down to the costume shop. He picked out a white jacket, black pants, bow tie, and white shoes. I found a strapless flowered cotton dress and a pink sweater with an antique sweater clip, and I completed the look with white canvas tennies, ankle socks, a bouffant hairdo with a pink scarf tied in the back, and a single strand of pearls. My husband wore a pink carnation boutonniere on his lapel and I had a fresh flower corsage on my wrist. We definitely looked the part and were ready to rock at the 50s dance.

Well, ready to rock might be exaggerating just a bit. My husband and I had plenty of enthusiasm and desire to rock, but we really weren't very good dancers. When disco was in, we took dance lessons at Arthur Murray, so we figured if we stood on the dance floor at least twelve inches apart and each of us did our own disco-dancing thing, we'd probably look respectable. But, if at any point during the night we were required to actually touch each other and slow dance, we were in big trouble.

I suggested to my husband that we practice slow dancing before going to the party, and he thought it was a good idea. So in our living room, two hours before the big dance, Tony Bennett was in the background leaving his heart in San Francisco, and my husband and I were doing our best to two-step, three-step, box-step—anything that looked remotely close to dancing. But soon (too soon) it was time to go.

It was an impressive-looking party. The band sounded great, people were already dancing when we arrived, and waiters circled the floor holding trays of fancy hors d'oeuvres high up in the air. At first my husband and I felt a little awkward on the dance floor, but it was crowded, so no one noticed us. We were actually starting to have a lot of fun when suddenly the music stopped. Our hostess took the microphone and said that she had planned on having everyone vote for a King and Queen of the dance, but after seeing one couple's outfits, there was no doubt as to who should be crowned.

"Suzanne and Bob Beecher, would you please take the dance floor and dance the first slow dance as reigning King and Queen?"

This can't be happening. Were those our names I heard? People were clapping and looking at us, waiting for my husband and me to take the dance floor. A slow dance? The two of us slow dancing with everyone at the party watching? I'd always dreamed of being Prom Queen . . . but this felt like a nightmare.

We had no choice. The music started, my husband put his arm around me, our feet started to shuffle, and somehow we were moving around the floor. Well, we were barely moving, but at least we weren't stepping on each other's feet. I'm sure people watching thought we were playing up the part, as we gazed into each other's eyes, but really it was panic. I whispered to my husband, "Thank heavens we practiced. Do you realize how stupid we'd look if we hadn't?"

It was the longest song I'd ever heard. Halfway through I invited the other guests to join us on the dance floor. Finally my husband and I could go back to our two-step shuffling in the midst of the crowd.

Most of us wish for a happy ending to every story, and in the end, the 50s dance (our solo slow dance included), turned out to be a dream come true. My prince charming held me in his shaking arms and in the midst of our slow shuffle around the floor, he whispered in my ear, "Suzanne, you're my dream come true and I love you."

The second invitation was two months after my father died, when I was home visiting my mom. Some of her friends stopped by and invited us out to dinner. They were going to the Elmo Club, and afterward they were heading to the big senior dance in Platteville to listen to the Busch's Swing Band.

My mother immediately declined, insisting it was too soon for her to be seen out in public. But I knew that the alternative was the two of us sitting in the living room watching television and sharing a liverwurst sandwich. So I coaxed Mom along, reminding her how much I loved to go to the Elmo Club. My parents used to take me there when I was a kid and my dad always ordered a kiddy cocktail for me.

"Couldn't we just go for an early dinner, Mom, and then come right home?"

She finally agreed.

I knew all of the women sitting around the table because most of them were moms of the kids I used to play with, and if I didn't show up on time for dinner, my mother would call looking for me. The seventy-eight-year-old woman sitting across from me was one of my high-school teachers. So it did feel a little strange at first switching roles, but there we were having dinner together, all talking on the same level as if it had always been that way.

The Elmo Club didn't disappoint me. The food was just as good as I remembered it being thirty-some years ago, though I didn't order my usual kiddy cocktail. Yes, it was a great idea going out to dinner. Mom looked a lot more relaxed, until someone mentioned the dance again. But before my mother could refuse, there was kind of a group intervention. All of Mom's friends were widowed, too, and they knew she needed a real night out. So after more coaxing we were all on our way to the dance.

The parking lot was full and buses were dropping off seniors near the front door. It was a huge dance hall, decorated with crepe paper and balloons. A sign on the way in read: GET YOUR NAME TAG AND SIGN UP FOR DOOR PRIZES! We were lucky; we found a big round table near the front. The band had already started playing, but no one was dancing. I was thinking, *This is pretty much like the beginning of every dance I've ever gone to. Who is going to be the first couple on the dance floor?*

Two songs later, when the slow beat changed to a swing, the first couple, two women who must have been in their late seventies, braved the dance floor. Hands clasped together, not the least bit concerned—all eyes were on them—they held the dance floor alone, and when the song finished they stayed put, anticipating the next number. But when the music started again, couples (mostly women dancing with women) flooded the dance floor. "If you want to dance," one of my mother's friends advised, "you'd better not wait around for a man to ask, because there aren't enough of them to go around."

I noticed my mother tapping her foot and there was a remnant of a smile on her face when she leaned over and whispered to me, "May I please have this dance?"

Now it was a very strange thing to be dancing with my mother. At first I just stood on the dance floor staring at the five-foot-tall woman, my dancing partner, my mother—whom I'd never, ever seen dance before. I was shocked. Who was this woman? Her hips swaying side to side, shoulders loose, keeping time to the music. Just when did my mother learn how to do this? I had no idea how to do these dance moves, but it didn't matter. The next thing I knew, my mother took me by the hand and I was twirling around the dance floor. I could have sworn her dark brown hair was pulled back in a ponytail, and she was sporting white bobby socks and saddle shoes.

Breathless and a bit stunned, I started walking back to our table when the song was over, but instantly the music started again and so did my mother. We danced another dance, and another dance, and another dance.

After that—it was all kind of a blur, and finally when the music moseyed its way into a slow song, I was so thankful, thinking I'd finally get to sit one out.

But my mother stood her ground, grabbing my elbows and then gently looking into my eyes, letting me know that for whatever reason, she had to keep dancing. Then she slid her arm around my back, our hands came together, my mother closed her eyes, and some of her sadness melted into a smile as we glided around the floor.

It was the most memorable dance of my life. Slow dancing with my mother.

Recipes Me, Myself, and I Dared to Try— AND We're So Glad We Did!

I've never been a big fan of zucchini (too many bad zucchini memories from my childhood). I have a lot of great memories about growing up in a small town, but zucchini season is not one of them. Every year when the first homegrown zucchini was spotted, word spread quickly and the friendly community where I lived suddenly became a ghost town. The small-town dwellers locked their doors, pulled the drapes, and hid in fear until the zucchini plague had passed over.

Gardens are plentiful in a small town and so is their bounty—especially zucchini. Each zucchini seed packet contains about forty seeds and no respectable gardener can seem to resist planting each and every one of them. If it were any other vegetable you could count on casualties, so things would even themselves out, but not with zucchini.

Zucchini have got the vegetable procreation thing down pat. Plant those forty seeds in lousy soil, ignore them, deprive them of fertilizer, but as long as the sun shines and it rains, they'll grow . . . and grow . . . and grow. And that's the problem. Zucchini bread and cake, stuffed zucchini, grilled zucchini pizza, chocolate zucchini slices, zucchini and cream cheese sandwiches. Enough already.

So when my friend Linda cooked a birthday lunch for me and the first course was Zucchini Bisque, I ate it only to be polite. But to my surprise the bisque was fantastic—actually, now I rave it's the best soup I've ever tasted. I think you'll like it, too.

Zucchini Bisque

Serves 4

2 tablespoons butter
1 medium onion, coarsely chopped
1 cup chopped carrots
4 cups coarsely chopped zucchini
1 can chicken broth (or one bouillon cube dissolved in 1 cup boiling water)
¼ teaspoon marjoram
¼ teaspoon sugar, optional
¼ cup cream or milk, optional
For garnish: nutmeg, fresh parsley

Melt butter in a large saucepan over medium heat and add vegetables. Cook until onions are limp. Stir in broth, marjoram, and sugar (if using). Simmer for 20 minutes until vegetables are tender.

Cool slightly, then mix into a pulp till smooth. Add ¼ cup cream or milk, if using, and return to heat till warm. Serve garnished with nutmeg and parsley.

You can freeze the bisque before adding cream or milk. I freeze portions in sandwich bags.

The soup is great served cold, but I like it warm.

Company Fare Pork Chops

This is a recipe that I found in my Grandma Hale's old recipe box. It's written out on a 3 x 5 recipe card in her handwriting, and there's a note she added before the recipe: "Don't shy away from this recipe, absolutely delicious! Can be prepared in advance just as well as not."

Grandma's last note: "Don't plan on serving six people with this recipe. It is too good—people will want more than a second helping."

6 thick pork chops
12 small white onions
5 tart apples, peeled and quartered
½ cup raisins, parboiled until plump
1 tablespoon brown sugar
1 cup beef consommé
Salt, pepper, nutmeg, clove, bay leaf, parsley (no notation of how much, I
   just sprinkle some over the top)

Brown pork chops on both sides and then place in a small roaster or a deep casserole.

Arrange onions and apples over them, and then add raisins and sprinkle with brown sugar.

Add consommé (not diluted), salt, and pepper, and then sprinkle the other spices over the entire thing. Cover tightly and cook at 350 degrees for 1½ hours.

Chicken Crepes

They are divine!

This recipe sounds like a big deal to make, but it's not. The first time I tried it I was afraid because of the crepes. I'd never made any and figured it would be too difficult. The first few crepes I made were too big, but then I quickly got the hang of it and you will, too. People will think you were in the kitchen cooking all day long when you make this!

Serves 6 or 7

12 crepes (see page 156)
2 (10-ounce) packages broccoli spears frozen in butter sauce
¼ cup flour
1½ cups water
1 tablespoon instant chicken bouillon
1 cup shredded Cheddar cheese
2 tablespoons sour cream
2 tablespoons sherry
1 tablespoon minced fresh parsley
Dash onion salt
Dash pepper
1½ cups cubed cooked chicken or turkey
2½-ounce jar sliced mushrooms, drained, or fresh mushrooms
¼ cup grated Parmesan cheese

First make the crepes and set aside. Cook broccoli according to package directions. Snip corner of pouches and drain butter sauce into medium saucepan. Stir in flour until smooth. Add water and bouillon and heat, stirring constantly, until thickened and smooth. Stir in ½ cup Cheddar cheese, the sour cream, sherry, parsley, and onion salt and pepper; heat until cheese is melted. Add chicken and mushrooms.

Preheat oven to 350 degrees.

Place a broccoli spear on each crepe. Top with 1 to 2 tablespoons of chicken sauce. Fold crepes and place seam side up in 13 x 9-inch baking dish. Pour remaining sauce over crepes. Sprinkle with remaining ½ cup Cheddar cheese and Parmesan cheese. Bake for 20 minutes.

Basic Crepes

4 eggs
¼ teaspoon salt
2 cups all-purpose flour
2⅓ cups milk
¼ cup oil

In large bowl, beat eggs and salt until foamy. Lightly spoon flour into measuring cup and level off. Add flour and milk to the eggs and beat well. Add oil and beat until well blended.

Heat small 7- or 8-inch skillet over medium-high heat. A few drops of water sprinkled on the pan will sizzle and bounce when heat is just right. Grease pan lightly with oil. Pour about 3 tablespoons of batter into pan, tilting pan to spread evenly. When crepe is light brown and set, turn to brown other side. Remove from pan. Adding oil as necessary, repeat with remaining batter. Stack cooked crepes, putting wax paper or parchment paper in between. You can freeze any extra crepes.

15. I Miss My Mother

My mother and I were clowns in the annual Cuba City parade, and we even won a prize two years in a row.

Love isn't always a guarantee between a mother and a daughter, at least it wasn't for my mother and me. We cared for each other, but I think it was more out of a sense of duty. So it was very difficult, twice a year, when I found myself standing in front of rows of greeting cards, agonizing over which birthday or Mother's Day card to buy.

I couldn't bring myself to give my mother a card thanking her for her love and affection, or for how special she made me feel. But I also didn't want to send a generic "Happy Day" card that might suggest how I really felt about our relationship. I guess a daughter always holds out hope—who knows, maybe it was that way for my mother, too.

Was I the only daughter who felt this way? When I asked my friend Linda, she was sympathetic but didn't offer any advice on how to change my relationship with my mother, or about which card to buy. But she did and I tried to hide my trembling hands. I thought it was her. She looked just like my mother. But of course it couldn't be my mother. My headphones, where are my headphones? I turned the music on loud and then louder, thinking maybe I could transport myself somewhere else. It was all too much for me.

Every Wednesday I have an appointment with my hairdresser. I don't even own a bottle of shampoo, and my mother's to blame. Yes, my mother who washed out every container: "Throw nothing away, buy nothing unless it's on sale, buy the wrong size and make it fit, if it's a good price." Oh, how many times did I hear those words? Yet Mom had a standing weekly appointment at the hairdresser. In fact, I don't ever remember seeing my mother wash and dry her own hair—not even once.

The small-town price of a weekly wash and blow-dry, and a monthly tint, was somehow justifiable in Mom's self-imposed budget. Maybe it was because she always worked a full-time job, or maybe my mother was like me—I can't blow-dry my hair into anything that looks even remotely respectable.

The first year Mom and Ron came to winter in Florida, my mother gasped when I took her along to my weekly hair appointment. Thirty dollars for a wash and blow-dry, fifty dollars for a haircut. My mother was beside herself, but it was one of the few times in her life she decided to take a chance.

"Go ahead and cut my hair," Mom told my hairdresser. "Make me look beautiful."

An hour later I barely recognized my mother. She became a different woman that day and she had a special smile—it was the same smile I was looking at now across the room. Oh, how I wish the woman with the tint on her hair was my mother, even for a minute—just a hug, an embrace, just to feel my mother's arms around me again.

But all I could do was stare. I walked away until the woman was out of sight, thinking maybe I was imagining things. But when I returned, she was still there and so was that smile. A smile from across the room—a smile meant just for me, to tuck away in my heart.

I miss my mother.

After my mother died, a close friend of mine gave me permission to grieve for as long as it took. She knew I needed to hear those words because I was frightened—afraid that I'd never find my way back. But one morning, almost a year and a half later, when I woke up things were different. I missed my mother, but now when I said those words, I was at peace and I felt different. The pain was gone.

Grieving had been a long journey. I realized that it didn't end that day, that it would never end, but the road before me had changed. I could see the lights; I could see a new wonderment in the world. Now when I looked at other people smiling, I didn't wonder anymore *What's wrong with them, don't they know how sad life is? Don't they know the world has come to an end because I miss my mother?*

The days and months, when would this pain end? How could it ever go away? Stories about my mother—I used to think about them over and over again, but they only made me miss her even more; the last words we said to each other; the day my mother pulled a magazine off the rack in the supermarket, opened it, and proudly announced to everyone, "That's my daughter on page thirteen." The afternoon my mother sat beside me on the sofa and told me she was going to have to leave, but she knew I'd be all right. I was a good girl and she loved me. Those stories used to bring me to my knees, but now they comforted me.

Yes, things were different now. The grip on my heart was now an embrace. I could breathe. I felt joy. My mother was right. I will be okay.

But still . . . *I miss my mother.*

My Mother's Oatmeal Chocolate-Chip Cookies

Baking chocolate-chip cookies and giving them away is something I do for fun. Friends, neighbors, and even business associates refer to me as "the Cookie Woman." I used to think giving away cookies was my own idea, but apparently it's in my genes.

My mother never enjoyed cooking. So I was really surprised when I was standing in the receiving line at her wake, and after people offered their sympathies, they said they'd never forget my mother because she was always baking cookies and giving them away. I was amazed. All those years, I guess my mother and I had more in common than we realized.

Mom's specialty was Oatmeal Chocolate-Chip cookies. Here's a copy of her recipe I found when I was digging through her old recipe box.

1½ cups all-purpose flour
1 teaspoon baking soda
1 teaspoon salt
1 cup butter
1 cup granulated sugar
1 cup light brown sugar
2 eggs
1 teaspoon pure vanilla extract
3 cups oatmeal
chocolate chips (my mother never indicated how many, but I use 1 to 2 cups)

Preheat oven to 375 degrees.

Mix the flour, baking soda, and salt together. Mix remaining ingredients together with the flour mixture and then add the chocolate chips.

Bake for 10 to 12 minutes until cookies are light brown. (Cool and then give them away to friends, neighbors, and strangers.)

Ron's Goulash

My mother didn't like to cook, but Ron did. In fact, he's a great cook. Ron's shy about his cooking talents, because he says "there's nothing to my recipes." They may be simple to make, but they sure do taste good. Here's one of his favorites and mine, too.

2 pounds hamburger
1 medium onion, chopped
8 ounces elbow macaroni
1 (15-ounce can) Hunt's tomato sauce
1 can cut green beans, optional
Salt and pepper to taste
Clove garlic, crushed, optional

Brown the hamburger and onion together. Meanwhile, cook macaroni per directions on package. Mix rest of ingredients together with hamburger and macaroni and simmer until it smells good enough to eat.

16. Still In-a-Pickle and It's <u>Not</u> What Miss Manners Would Do

Rolling my own dough and baking pies is a messy job, but it's so relaxing.

"SHHH!! It's a Surprise Party! For Kiki on May 6th at 7 p.m."

The party invitation addressed to me included an address and a phone number, so I could RSVP, but the invite didn't say who was throwing the party for Kiki—not that it mattered—because I had a much bigger problem . . . WHO THE HECK IS KIKI?

Obviously a good friend of Kiki's sent me the invitation, because she thinks I'm also a good friend of Kiki's. But now I feel like I'm really losing my mind, because I'm supposed to be good friends with two people I don't know: the party giver and the party girl. Why else would I get an invitation, but . . . WHO THE HECK IS KIKI?

It was amusing for a while, receiving an invitation to a party where I didn't recognize any names or the address, and when I drove by the house I was certain I'd never seen it before in my life. To save my sanity, I started questioning my friends (friends I was absolutely certain I knew) to see if they knew a friend, or if we know a friend, or if anyone knows a friend of a friend—could anyone help me? But they all just wanted to know "WHO THE HECK IS KIKI?"

"Pick up the phone and just ask," my real friends suggested. But how do I call an unknown *someone* who invited me to a party for *our* dear friend Kiki, and casually inquire, "Who are you and . . . WHO THE HECK IS KIKI?"

It would be very embarrassing if the reply was "What's wrong with you, Suzanne? Of course you know Kiki! We all had lunch together last week. Don't you remember you ordered the chicken salad?"

So I asked my daughter-in-law to make the call instead. Her story (well, the lie we made up, because if there was ever a time to lie this was it) was that the postman had delivered the invitation to her by mistake, and she thought she'd better call to let someone know it went to the wrong address. And of course, then she'd get the chance to ask that ever burning question, "WHO THE HECK IS KIKI?" and the mystery would be solved.

But that's not what happened. Instead, things took a nasty turn.

The woman curtly interrupted my daughter-in-law. "Why are you bothering me? You shouldn't have opened the invitation. If you don't know who Kiki is, the invitation obviously wasn't meant for you, and I'd certainly never invite anyone like you to the party."

"WHO THE HECK IS KIKI?"

Nobody really cares anymore.

But my daughter-in-law and I are dying to meet Kiki's pretentious friend. What was the date and time of that party?

Kiki's getting two new friends for her birthday.

(Don't worry, the name and date in this recipe from my life was changed to protect the smarty-pants! I ended up not going to the party because I came down with a bad cold, and I figured even Kiki didn't deserve that for her birthday.)

Door-to-Door Etiquette

Dark suit, white shirt, dark tie, and a book and pamphlets tucked underneath his arm. I knew right away who he was, and what he wanted the minute I spotted the "tools" of his trade. So after he delivered his opening line, I butted in and suggested we just cut right to the chase.

I explained that normally he'd want to show me "the way" and then I'd try to tell him that I was already taken care of in that department, but nevertheless, he'd still keep right on talking, because he doesn't like "my way" and eventually I'd politely shut the door in the middle of his sentence.

"So here's the thing," I told him, "my writing muse is on vacation and it's been kind of tough going today. You see, when I get to a certain point in a column, I usually call my writing muse and she listens to me talk. And since I'm without someone to listen to me today, and you're here, and you want to talk and hang around my front porch anyway, how about if you listen to me talk about my column and then it will be your turn to talk, and I'll listen. Have we got a deal?"

And before he could realize what he'd agreed to, I pulled up a lawn chair and told him to sit down and put his feet up. "Do you want a glass of lemonade? I think we might be here awhile. I can't quite decide on a lead."

Line by line, I delivered my column and he even laughed in the places I was hoping for at least a giggle. But when I got near the end and I was starting to stumble, because I still needed to do some rewriting, he started getting impatient. He looked down at his watch and when I heard him clear his throat, I was afraid that Persuader Man was going to try to slide in one of his "this is the way" lines. So I just kept right on going at the end of my sentence, rolling right over the period, not even stopping to take a breath. Then I slid right into the next sentence, and when my substitute muse's attention started to wane even more, I reminded him that we had an agreement.

"Doesn't it say something in that 'persuasion' book you're totin' around about keeping your side of a bargain?"

I give him credit. Persuader Man sat back down, and he was a pretty good listener—he didn't have too many creative suggestions, but then again that wasn't part of our deal. And soon it was his turn. But by then, the sweat was running down his face (it was 98 degrees even in the shade), and in all fairness, he'd probably forgotten his lines because I'd interrupted his usual presentation flow.

"Not to worry," I told him. "My muse takes two vacations a year. Give me your card and the next time she leaves town, I'll call you."

All You Can Eat . . . If All You Can Eat is One Bite

Every invention comes from necessity, and whoever invented the garbage disposal must have been inspired by a mother and 125 miniature white Styrofoam containers from a senior meal site.

When my mother died three years ago, it was very difficult to pack up her things and find a home for them. However, it was not difficult to haul 125 Styrofoam containers out to the curb for Tuesday's trash pickup.

Mom didn't enjoy cooking, so after Dad passed away she started having lunch at the senior meal site in the small town where she lived. It was the perfect cooking solution. Not only did Mom get a hot lunch every day, but because she started volunteering, she got to take home leftovers—food that would have been thrown out anyway. In theory, this all sounded wonderful. The problem was when I'd visit Mom, she'd never let me take her out to dinner.

"Why waste food?" Mom would reply when I'd extend an invitation. "There's roast beef, turkey pot pie, scalloped potatoes, coleslaw, corn, fruit salad, and cherry cobbler in the refrigerator for dinner."

I admit, it sounded like a smorgasbord; she must have been cooking like crazy anticipating my visit. So I started setting the dining room table for a fancy feast, but my mother started lining up fifteen little miniature Styrofoam containers on the kitchen counter. Taking the lids off the containers one by one, Mom took my order for the evening's fare: "What would you like? How about a little of everything?"

Yeah, boy, that's what it was going to have to be. Because there was one bite of roast beef in one container, maybe three bites of turkey pie in another, six kernels of corn in yet another, and five miniature containers with dabs of cherry cobbler—enough to actually make one dessert. But whose dinners were all of these miniature containers left over from? I could only hope they were my mother's. Bon appétit!

My mother grew up in the "waste not . . ." era. So I knew the only way to get rid of the Styrofoam leftovers was either to eat them or get up early before she did, switch on the radio to drown out the sound, and then turn on the garbage disposal. "Mom, I ate the rest of the leftovers for breakfast, so we'll have to go out to dinner this evening."

I used to feel a bit guilty about tossing out my mother's Styrofoam collection after she passed away, but I'm pretty certain there's no use for Styrofoam in heaven. It's true you can't take it with you—but if you're like my mother—you'll drag it along as far as the front door of the Pearly Gates, and then you have to lay your bag of Styrofoam containers down.

And when you lay it down, I like to think that it's someone like my mother who is in charge of finding a good home for all those little containers. After all, you never know when you'll need a pint-size Styrofoam container that used to have a single serving of baked beans in it.

Even Miss Manners Would Lie

I was in the tub, the telephone rang, and the next thing I knew my husband was handing the phone to me. "Who is it?" I whispered.

My husband shook his head and mouthed, "I don't know." My dear husband is very uncomfortable lying to people, so he gets flustered when the phone rings and the caller asks for me. What's he to say? "Suzanne can't come to the phone, she's in the tub," or "Suzanne told me to tell anyone who calls that she's not here." The phone becomes a game of Hot Potato, my husband quickly handing it off and hoping it doesn't circle back around to him.

The woman on the other end of the line said, "Hello, this is Christine and I'm calling from the church. I'd like to know if you want to get your picture taken for the directory."

"No. Thank you very kindly, but I'll pass," I told her.

"Well, are you still a member?" she asked.

"Yes, I am."

"It doesn't cost anything to get your picture taken."

"I appreciate that, but I would really rather not. My life is kind of complicated right now."

"Well, okay, thanks anyway. Good-bye."

After I hung up the phone my first thought was *What have things come to? Why did I say that? I wonder what that woman is thinking now.* If I asked someone to do something and they told me, "No thank you, my life is kind of complicated right now," I would assume something awful—somebody died, someone was ill, or they were in the early stages of a nervous breakdown. But everything's A-OK in my life, so what's up? Before I could further analyze my mysterious reply, another thought popped into my head, one that was even more disturbing.

I started thinking about my old high-school yearbook, and then I got to worrying about what they'd print in the church directory. I can't remember exactly what the yearbook staff said the year Danny Coohn's picture was missing, but it went something like: "Danny's picture isn't here because he was expelled from school for two weeks, so he couldn't come on school grounds to get his picture taken."

Oh no! I can see it now: "Suzanne Beecher is not listed in this year's church directory because she was taking a bath when we called, and she told us her life was too complicated. We're all praying that her bath is successful and that her life uncomplicates very soon."

Gotta, Have-to, Even in the Pew

The minister was in the middle of his Sunday sermon and when he mentioned "Robert's Rules of Order"—well, that did it. Words started popping into my mind, coming at me fast and furiously. One after another, I couldn't stop them. Pretty soon the words were forming sentences, and the sentences were lining up like jets on the tarmac waiting their turn for takeoff. I had to get this stuff out of my mind. I didn't have any choice. I had to write a column then and there.

I always carry a notebook with me, but I was nervous about getting it out because my son and daughter-in-law, who are usually sitting in the pew next to me, said that the last time I received so-called divine writing inspiration, I was oblivious to the commotion I created. You see, sometimes when I write, the ideas come so quickly and I'm so completely engrossed in the words that I'm unaware what's going on around me. Apparently, the single sheet of paper and the stubby pencil that I was using that particular day were crinkling so loudly that people were turning around and staring at me. I do remember my son giving me the evil eye to stop, but I thought he was just passing judgment on whether or not I should be writing a column in the midst of a church service.

So this time I gently and quietly (*shhh . . .*) pulled my notebook out of my purse, softly clicked the end of the pen, and when I started writing, I listened—spot-checking for sound effects—heard nothing, and it was my turn for takeoff.

By the time the minister finished his story, I'd finished mine, too, and

I discreetly put away my tools. But in the middle of the following prayer, two more thoughts that were the perfect finishing touch for my story were begging to be written down—I couldn't resist. I mean, who would know? Every dutiful praying person should have his eyes closed and head bowed, right? Anyone who didn't—and could see me writing—well, it was kind of like getting caught doing something you shouldn't, by someone else who was doing the same thing. So you're both in deep doo-doo and neither one of you will fess up. And we didn't.

Chicken Scratches

I was on the phone talking with an author about his book and hurriedly jotting down every word he said. But when I tried to read his quotes back to him, I was stumbling over the words in front of me. I couldn't read my own handwriting, or as my friend Hilda would call it, "chicken scratches."

Hilda is ninety-five-plus years old. She's a friend of mine, and when I went to the market the other day, she came along. When she pulled out her shopping list, I noticed it looked like it had been drafted in the middle of an earthquake. We were both laughing about it and simply decided that things can get a little shaky with age.

I told Hilda not to worry or feel one little bit embarrassed about her handwriting, because it happens to me, too. Sometimes when I have an idea for a column, especially if I'm on the run, I grab whatever I can and quickly jot my thoughts down. It's always a relief to know that my idea is safely written down, so I let it wander out of my mind. But unfortunately, the next day when I try to type up my notes, it's all a mystery to me. I can read only about every third word. And some sentences are totally lost in translation, because my writing is as cryptic as Hilda's shopping list. Assuming each line on the shopping list was a separate item, Hilda and I decided there were twenty words we needed to decode, so we started at the top.

"Okay, Hilda, this looks kind of like a *p*, doesn't it? And it appears to be a long word, so let's see, what do you think?"

"Pepper? Potatoes?" (No, her neighbor brought six potatoes over yesterday morning.)

"Popcorn? Hilda, do you think it's popcorn?"

Yes! That was it! One down! (Hilda remembered she ran out of popcorn Thursday night while she was watching her favorite TV show.)

And with the skill of two veteran *Wheel of Fortune* players, down the list we went, letter by letter, item by item. By the third entry on our list, the shoppers around us must have thought we'd both lost our minds. Practically yelling back and forth—Hilda's a little hard of hearing—we'd be exchanging guesses.

"This one looks like it's eggs, Hilda, but it starts with a *d*."

"Do you want to buy a vowel?"

"Gimme an *e* for $250, Pat. Spin that wheel for us, Vanna."

A *d* and an *e*. Eggo waffles? No, I bet it's a dozen eggs.

"Do you need a dozen eggs, Hilda?"

I do believe it was the most entertaining shopping trip either of us had been on in a long time. Now, if I could just decipher the chicken scratches in front of me. What did that author say again? It looks like it starts with a *g*, but it could be a *p* . . . maybe I need to buy a vowel, or call Hilda?

Hurry, Wrap It Up So I Can Write

I should never, ever go to the market when I'm hungry. It can be disastrous. Everything looks so inviting to a hungry woman. When I walk into the market (my stomach growling), the first place I head for is the deli counter, where they slice the meat and cheese to order. I take a number and wait patiently, but I don't mind because I'll be rewarded with the first slice.

"Is this thin enough for you, ma'am?" The clerk gently raises the corner of the sliced ham for my inspection and then the question my stomach's been waiting to hear, "Would you like to try a slice?"

It's a repeat performance when he slices my cheese and other deli requests. By the time I move on to another department, I've pretty much curbed my appetite and I can shop without fear of any hunger-induced impulse buys.

Another thing I should never, ever do is go to the market without my notebook and pen. While I was waiting for my deli order to be filled, I felt the urge to start writing a column. But I didn't have anything to write on, except the butcher paper wrapped around my thinly sliced Baby Swiss. No complaints, though, it was the perfect palette, quite inspiring really—a big wide open white space to write on. But when I went to check out and handed over the Baby Swiss package to be scanned, I realized from the cashier's look that I'd better give her an explanation, and fast!

"Don't worry, it's not a stickup note," I said, trying to smile and hold my hands where she could clearly see them. "I'm just a writer who forgot to bring her notebook and this is tomorrow's column."

Ron and Virginia's Bread-and-Butter Pickles

My mother canned pickles when I was a kid, but my mother's pickles weren't edible until she met Ron. Mom's pickles tasted like kerosene. But I never had the courage to tell her, because she proudly served her homemade pickles with every meal. I got real good at hiding them in a napkin and tossing them in the trash.

But when my mother married Ron, not only did she discover the love of her life, he came with a tasty pickle recipe, too. These are fabulous Bread-and-Butter Pickles.

1 gallon cucumbers
8 small white onions
2 green peppers, shredded, if you want
½ cup canning salt
1 quart cracked ice

the table—that was okay with him. Three? No way. He was concerned that inviting that extra third person might mean no leftovers for him.

People do indeed get serious about leftovers and if it looks like there might not be any, they take matters into their own hands. Mom loved my shrimp salad and every year when she'd come to my house for Thanksgiving dinner, she'd gobble up at least three helpings right away. Then she'd spend the rest of the meal keeping tabs on anyone who headed back to the kitchen for seconds. Following close behind, Mom would do her best to encourage them to eat more turkey, mashed potatoes, or coleslaw—anything other than the shrimp salad because she wanted to take home the leftovers. However when my husband and I went to my mother's house for Thanksgiving dinner—no leftovers for us. And here's the reason why.

The first year Grandma Hale passed the Thanksgiving dinner rite of passage preparation on to my mother, she fixed a pretty tasty meal. But then Mom started dieting and the menu got down to basics—basically our dinner now involved my mother opening a can of peas and a box of mashed potatoes, putting a glob of cranberry sauce on a plate (still in the shape of the can it slid out of), and opening a package of white dinner rolls. The only thing that wasn't out of the can or the box was the bird.

I didn't want to complain about the food and hurt Mom's feelings, and in her defense, she really didn't enjoy cooking. So the following year, after the first instant out-of-the-box Thanksgiving, my husband and I offered to help her cook. We went to my mother's house the day before Thanksgiving, did almost all of the cooking ourselves, and then spent the night. We had a wonderful Thanksgiving meal, and my mother even commented on how good everything tasted. Before my husband and I headed back home, I asked Mom if we could take some leftovers with us and she matter-of-factly said "No."

I was shocked—no further explanation and no leftovers for us that Thanksgiving.

So the following year I suggested that perhaps it was time for Mom to pass the Thanksgiving dinner on to me. Thank heavens she agreed, so I took the bird and ran with it—not only would we be guaranteed a tasty Thanksgiving meal, but for sure we'd get leftovers. And just to make real sure there was plenty of food left over, my husband and I made two of everything that year: two turkeys, two batches of potatoes, gravy, vegetables, shrimp salad, double the number of deviled eggs, and we bought fourteen loaves of bread at the bakery. Everyone who came to our house for Thanksgiving dinner took home a leftover dinner, complete with a piece of homemade pie and their own loaf of bread.

The year of the leftovers left such an impression that I've considered extending the Thanksgiving celebration to two days. On Thursday everybody gets formally dressed for dinner (including the turkey) and then on Friday we all gather together again for a leftover dinner. Sitting at the Thanksgiving table in pantyhose and a form-fitting dress, I can't really do the original twenty-course holiday meal justice. But slide me into some stretchy, elastic-waisted pants on Leftover Day, slip on my flip-flops, twist my hair up and stick it under a baseball cap, and I could probably even go back for thirds on pumpkin pie topped with whipped cream.

When my husband and I moved from Wisconsin to Florida, we wanted to start a new Thanksgiving tradition to remind us of the first holiday we celebrated in the new chapter of our life. So the day before Thanksgiving we furiously shopped all of the antique stores in Sarasota looking for something for our Thanksgiving table. It was a quarter to five, the local shops were getting ready to close, and we'd pretty much given up hope of finding something. But the very last antique store we hurried into, there they were—antique Thanksgiving plates for our dinner table. "His Majesty's china plates Made in England." The rim of each plate hosted a cornucopia of fall vegetables and in the center there was a proud colorful turkey in a country setting. Mixing old and new traditions, I set the Thanksgiving table in our new historical home with Grandma Hale's pink water glasses, our new china turkey plates, and the wooden figurines from the year I taught a cooking class to homeschooled children.

Eight sixth-grade students enrolled in my cooking class, including Max. It was obvious that Max didn't want to be in my kitchen. He was tough looking, the kind of kid that would make you cross over to the other side of the street if you were out for a leisurely stroll. Ragged hair that always looked like it needed to be washed, baggy clothes, and oversized, steel-toed curb-stomping boots. In his mind, I'm sure Max thought he was lookin' cool.

He had been kicked out of every public and private school he'd been enrolled in and homeschooling was a last resort for his parents. I'm sure his folks were jumping for joy and would have gladly paid double the price when they saw my announcement—Six-Week Cooking Class for Home-schoolers—because it would give them a three-hour break during the day.

On the first day when we did introductions, I asked each student to tell me what they hoped to learn. Tough kid's response: "My parents made me come here. Sounds stupid to me."

Okay, I could work with that. Maybe.

But Max would never give an inch. It would have been giving in to the establishment to actually enjoy himself, even when he was eating a cream puff. "Well, what do you think? Do you like them?" I was hoping the fluffy white filling might force one crummy smile from him, but no . . . he was one tough cookie. Nevertheless, I genuinely liked the kid. I respected his pigheadedness. It reminded me of myself when I was his age.

Each student had kitchen assignments, but I never pressed Max to do much of anything, except I did enforce a "no smoking" rule during the three-hour class period. However, I'd still catch him smoking outside when we'd take a break. I spoke to his parents about it, but they just shrugged their shoulders: "What can you do?"

Max wasn't disrupting the class and the other kids accepted his behavior for what it was, so I figured no real harm done. Tough boy would try to follow a recipe every now and then, but he moved so slowly—to emphasize his disgust in being there—that by the time he'd get some cookie batter mixed up we were out of time.

The finale of the six-week cooking class was to prepare a holiday buffet for the kids' parents. Thanksgiving was only a couple of weeks away, so we decided to do a half-Thanksgiving, half-Christmas theme with the table decorations. All of the kids showed up for class early on the big day, including Max, which surprised me, because I wasn't sure he was going to show up at all. That's why I hadn't given him an assignment.

"Here, these are for the table," Max said, his eyes looking away from me. "I made them last night." And he handed me two wooden snowmen, two Christmas trees, and a Pilgrim and an Indian.

I was stunned—they were adorable. He'd hand-carved and painted them on all sides, so no matter where they sat on the buffet table you'd be able to see the detail of his work. You never know about people. I thought I was going to cry, but I could tell Max didn't want me to make too big of a deal about it. His parents were as shocked as I'd been when I pointed out what their son had made.

Two wooden Christmas trees, two snowmen, an Indian, and a Pilgrim sit on the shelf of my china closet, but every year on Thanksgiving and Christmas I take them down and put them in the center of my table, and of course I retell the story of the boy who made them for me.

Remembering Max's story has become a cherished holiday tradition, and when my husband is carving the turkey, we remember the year Mom attempted to solve the turkey-leg dilemma.

Some people want the white meat, some will only eat the dark, and for years our family used to argue over who was going to get a turkey drumstick. Every year it was the same routine. Mom would ring her china bell, "Dinner is ready. Come to the table." And we'd all start calling dibs on

eggnog, and pecan pie. Those were just a few of the in-between-meal snacks that Grandma always had in her house at Christmas time. But now there aren't even enough people in my family to eat all of those things, and nobody eats dip except me, and absolutely no one in our family eats pecan pie.

So why do I keep buying these things year after year, just to end up throwing most of them away? I don't understand it. I could buy these food items any time of the year if I wanted to, but I don't—not until they start piping Christmas music into the supermarket and then I head straight to the chip-and-dip aisle and off to the bakery in search of a pecan pie.

Maybe the reason I keep buying things that nobody eats anymore is because I'm missing the person who used to love to eat them. My Grandpa Hale loved pecan pie. His birthday was the day before Christmas and he'd start eating pecan pie on the 24th, and continue eating pecan pie right up until New Year's Day. It was his once-a-year treat. Years after Grandpa passed away, my mother was still making his favorite pie, even though nobody would eat it, and I've continued the tradition. I don't know if I'm quite ready to give up the pecan pie, but I am making a little progress. Grandpa Hale also loved chocolate-covered cherries. Usually I buy two boxes, but last year I walked right by them.

Holiday traditions are very comforting and I want to continue them, but I also leave a little wiggle room. For years I raised my right hand and took the oath: "I'll never ever have an artificial Christmas tree!" and I believed every word of it. But then a couple of years go when my husband and I walked by the almost-real Christmas trees on display, there was a moment when in unison we looked at each other and said, "This tree looks real." And we bought it! Let me tell you, when I fall, I fall hard. I blush when I confess that the artificial tree already had lights on it, too.

My new eight-foot evergreen Christmas tree came in three easy-toassemble pieces; all I had to do was style it. Imagine that, I'm now a pine-tree stylist! Pull this branch to the right, move that one a little over to the left, give it a little tummy tuck to cover up the wide-open spaces, and twenty minutes later my tree looked just the way it did the year before—only there was no need to water it and I wouldn't have to vacuum up those messy pine needles. My only Christmas tree worry from now on was going to be how to get the eight-foot evergreen tree back into the little box it came in.

There's a lot of stigma concerning Christmas tree etiquette. In fact, there seems to be an unwritten law that if you put your tree up before Thanksgiving, you might as well be wearing white shoes in January. Most tree sinners are hush-hush about their transgressions and they walk around silently carrying some pretty heavy pine-tree guilt. But for others the shame is just too much to bear and they feel the need to confess.

Three weeks before Thanksgiving my manicurist leaned over and whispered to me, "I've had three Christmas trees up in my house for a week already and they're decorated, too. What do you think about that?"

I assured her not to worry, that her secret was safe with me, and then I made my own confession about how I'd taken the oath: "I'll never, ever have an artificial Christmas tree!" Yet hidden away in my bedroom closet was an eight-foot tree stuffed into a little cardboard box waiting to be styled. Yes, I too was a Christmas tree sinner! And if only I'd fallen from grace a few years earlier, I wouldn't have ruined the brand-new light gray carpeting in my living room.

We'd just moved into a new house and I wanted our Christmas tree decorations to complement the soft, warm colors of my new sofa, rug, and drapes. So I didn't bother getting out the Christmas boxes with our old favorites that year, because they just wouldn't do. Instead, I spent hours, actually days (I got a little obsessed), looking for light pink, dark pink, and cream-colored ornaments and matching lights to make a perfectly color-coordinated Christmas tree.

Yes, indeed, when I finished decorating my Christmas tree it was breathtaking. An all-pink masterpiece—but only on the front of the tree. The tree stood in the corner of the living room and I neglected to decorate the backside. And one afternoon, plop! Over the tree went! Broken ornaments scattered everywhere and the water that had tree preservative in it spilled out onto my new light gray carpeting. I was so angry at the tree and myself that I just let the stupid thing lie in the middle of the living room floor for two days, which of course set a water stain in the carpet. My family thought I'd lost my mind. Looking back, I'd have to agree.

The decorations I traditionally put on our Christmas tree have been accumulated over the years. Every ornament hanging on my Christmas tree reminds me of a story, and every year when I decorate my tree one by one I remember.

I remember the day my son came home from kindergarten and hurried into the living room to put the Life Savers yarn doll on the Christmas tree. "Look, Mom, see what I made." A miniature roll of Life Savers in the middle of yarn arms, legs, and long locks of golden hair. It's still holding up after all these years.

Three red rocking horses—my daughter begged me to buy them when she was seven years old; it was the same year she asked me about Santa.

Two pink drum ornaments, remnants of that "almost perfect" all-pink Christmas tree. I gave the rest of the unscathed pink- and cream-colored ornaments away (it was too embarrassing to keep them around). But I decided to keep two of the pink drums as a forever, humble reminder that I need to keep some balance in my life, especially during the holidays.

I'd forgotten all about it, but there it was at the bottom of the Christmas box. I remember the day Mom gave it to me, she was so thrilled to find it—a clown popping out of a wooden children's block with a V initial on the front of it. (V for Virginia, my mother's name.) Mom used to be a clown in her hometown parade in Cuba City, and one year I flew back home to be in the parade with her. We even won a prize. She gave me the Christmas ornament the year before she died.

That stupid clown—there it is waiting for me to hang it on the tree, but all I can do is cry and the crying turns into sobbing, my knees give way, and soon I'm sitting on the floor in front of the Christmas tree, crying and remembering, because every ornament on my tree tells a story, a recipe from my life that I hope I'll never forget.

Candy-Cane Cookies

This is one of my favorite Christmas cookie recipes. You can make candy canes red-and-white or red-and-green. People will think you spent a lot of time in the kitchen, but they're really simple to make. It's fun to braid the dough for the candy canes, but since I do it only once a year, the first two I make are usually gigantic, because I use too much dough. The cookies expand when they're baking, so I would make only two at first, as kind of a test run to get your candy-cane-cookie bearings. But not to worry, big candy-cane cookies taste just as great as small ones.

3½ cups flour
2 teaspoons baking powder
½ teaspoon salt
2 sticks butter, at room temperature
1¼ cups sugar
2 eggs beaten with 2 teaspoons vanilla extract
Red food coloring

Stir together the flour, baking powder, and salt in a bowl. Set aside.

Cream the butter and sugar. Add the egg mixture, a little at a time, beating well after each addition. Gradually add the flour mixture, blending well after each addition.

Put half of the dough in another bowl. Add red food coloring to one-half of dough to make the desired candy-cane shade. Leave the other half of dough plain. Shape each portion into a ball. Flatten each ball of dough, wrap snugly with plastic wrap, and refrigerate for 30 minutes or until slightly firm. Don't over-chill because then you won't be able to work with the dough.

Dust your hands and working surface with flour. Roll a one-inch ball of plain white dough into a rope about 6 inches long. Do the same with a red-colored piece of dough. Take the red-colored rope of dough, along with a plain piece of dough, and cross the red over the white, to make a candy cane. Shape one end of the crossed ropes into the head of a cane.

Bake in a 350-degree oven on greased cookie sheets for 12 to 14 minutes. The cookies may be a little soft when they come out of the oven. Let cool completely before you handle them.

18. Did Somebody Bring the Cookies?

Chocolate-chip cookies have become part of who I am. My business card reads: Suzanne Beecher, Writer/Cookie Baker.

Fun in the sun, year-round flower gardens, and white sandy beaches. After a year of renting a house on the water, my husband and I wondered what's not to love about living in Florida. So we made it official. We bought a 1926 historical home in Sarasota and applied for our Florida driver's licenses, which meant we were no longer "snowbirds," but official Floridians.

Living in Sarasota felt like a dream come true—big-city amenities, yet a little bit of small-town Cuba City. Main Street was only a ten-minute walk from our house. In fact, almost anywhere my husband and I wanted to go was within walking distance: the marina, library, market, theater, dry cleaner's, French bakery, restaurants, two coffeehouses, bookstore, live outdoor entertainment on a Saturday night, my doctor's office, even the hospital emergency room. So theoretically if I were home alone, fell off the kitchen stepstool, and blood wasn't gushing out too badly, I could probably hobble

Suzanne's Chocolate-Chip Cookies

Makes 36 cookies

2 sticks butter (make sure the butter is cold; slice it up before mixing)
¾ cup brown sugar
¾ cup granulated sugar
1 overflowing teaspoon pure vanilla extract
2 eggs
2¼ cups flour (plus an additional tablespoon if your kitchen is warm, or it's
  very humid outdoors)
1 teaspoon baking soda
1 teaspoon salt
2 overflowing cups good-quality chocolate chips

Beat together butter, brown and granulated sugars, and vanilla. Add eggs and combine well. In another bowl, mix together flour, baking soda, and salt.

Add flour mixture to butter mixture. Beat well. Add chocolate chips. Mix on low speed till just combined. Drop by teaspoons onto parchment-lined baking pans. Bake at 375 degrees for 10 to 12 minutes, until light golden brown.

Cool cookies on counter, then freeze immediately. I put the cookies into freezer bags. Freezing the cookies is an important step because it sets up the chocolate. When the cookie is thawed the chocolate stays firm.

Bake two batches, and give one away.

19. Seasonings: The Ingredients of a Small-Town Girl

My dog, Moochie, and me playing in the trailer lot. My parents and I lived in a trailer for a number of years while they were saving up money for a down payment on a house.

"It's better to be sad than happy. Too much happiness isn't good for anyone."

Years ago I heard a woman make that statement and it's stuck with me. Not because I thought it was something profound. In fact, at the time I thought the woman needed some serious help. But then a few years later, a friend of mine received some devastating news and as I was searching for words that might comfort her, I caught a little glimpse of what that woman might have been trying to convey.

Happiness is a wonderful thing and I definitely want my share. But if I'm really honest about it, the times in my life that have made me the person I am today have come from sadness. Knowing how to celebrate good news, how to hip-hip-hurray when the time is right, was standard equipment for me. Not much sorting needs to be done when the sun is shining, and I'm feeling great and problem free.

But finding the words to say to a friend who's going to have to shut down her business, or writing a note to someone whose younger sister just died from cancer, that kind of "knowing"—that kind of understanding—comes from the sadness I've experienced in my life.

I finally understood the woman's sentiments: "It's better to be sad than happy." No doubt about it, there's a purpose for both. I won't chase away the sadness; I might need it someday.

Yesterday when my husband and I were out for our morning walk, we stopped to read a poster that was tacked up on a telephone pole.

LOST CAT!

BROWN TABBY

MORRIS

20 YEARS OLD AND HARD OF HEARING

My husband commented that it was "that time of year," and Morris was probably just taking a romantic stroll around the neighborhood with a female companion. But the poster made me think about what happened to my dog, Moochie.

When I was five years old, Santa left Moochie under the Christmas tree. He was part terrier and part something else that must have had a very long tail, because when Moochie was just a pup, the veterinarian said we needed to shorten his tail or "the tail will grow longer than the dog." And so we had his tail nipped.

I was an only child, no brothers or sisters to play with except Moochie. Even when I'd dress him up in a pink dress and tie a ruffled bonnet around his neck, he was a real trouper. He'd ride in the side basket of my bicycle, barking nonstop—"Look at us"—and we'd go up and down Main Street. I loved that dog, but honestly I don't know how my parents put up with the pooch. Moochie loved to chew blankets. He never touched a shoe, sock, or a chair leg, but every single blanket in our house looked like a piece of Swiss cheese. Perfect little round holes—a real work of dog art—and every blanket, on every bed, was a Moochie masterpiece.

I never tied him up when he was outside, there wasn't any need to, because Moochie never left the yard. So it was strange one day when he just seemed to disappear. Everybody knew everybody and their pets in the small town I grew up in, but when I asked the neighbors, nobody had seen Moochie. Months went by, I was miserable, and I'd given up hope of ever finding him. The worst part was not knowing what had happened to him.

You know how things just seem to come together sometimes? There's no reason why a topic of conversation should come up, but it does when the time is right. That's what happened one day when I was waiting for my mother to get off work at the Dime Store.

It was almost five o'clock (closing time at the Dime Store) and Mom was behind the register ringing up the last customer when out of the blue, the woman she was waiting on, started telling a story about a dog who had wandered onto their farm a couple of months ago. It was a small brown dog, with a stump of a tail, and he just showed up one afternoon in their barn. He didn't look well and was obviously a very old dog, so the woman made a bed for him and tried to get him to eat, but he wasn't hungry. She'd been so worried about the dog that she got up in the middle of the night to check on him. The woman was in tears by that point in the story, and my mother and I were crying, too, because we realized who the dog was.

Moochie died in the woman's arms at about three in the morning.

Why did Moochie run away? I've always thought about it this way: Best friends never want to hurt each other, and I imagine Moochie decided it would be just too much for me—he wanted to spare me the pain, so he ran away from home to die.

LOST DOG!

BROWN, PART TERRIER WITH A SHORT TAIL

MOOCHIE

15 YEARS OLD AND THE BEST FRIEND I EVER HAD

I don't always recognize when I'm in the middle of a big moment, an experience that might change my life or someone else's. Perhaps it's a small gesture, a few simple words, or turning left instead of right. Maybe I was supposed to get lost this morning, maybe I was supposed to change my schedule and take a detour?

It's not an everyday event, but sometimes I feel an urgent tugging inside of me. Not a resounding call, rather more of a gentle nudge. In fact, if I ignored it long enough, it would move on and see if someone else was willing to help. I don't always know the person, nor do I have any idea what I'll be doing or saying when we meet, but it's clear from that little nudge that there's an opportunity waiting for me. The question is: Am I willing to listen and deviate from my comfortable routine? When I do find the courage, it's one of those perfect meant-to-be moments.

Years ago, I was headed home after a meeting and I noticed an elderly woman walking toward the bus stop, so I offered her a ride home. When we pulled up in front of her house, as I was helping her out of the car, I felt compelled to give her a hug. Without giving it a second thought I wrapped my arms around the woman and she held on tight, too. So very tight, yet the strangeness of our embrace neither one of us noticed.

"It's been years since my husband died, since someone has hugged me," she said, then she whispered a thank-you.

Who would have thought? The things I'm doing today. The words I'll say to someone tomorrow. Please, oh please, I want to remember they could be one of those big moments.

I'd stopped by a colleague's office for business advice and in the middle of a flurry of great ideas, he interrupted his thought midsentence. "I'm bipolar, did you know that?" He continued on with three or four more sentences about his bipolar disorder and how it affects him, and then returned to our original conversation.

I hadn't known about this man's disorder and I didn't mind hearing about it, but it seemed like a strange detour to take in the midst of a business conversation. But you know what was even stranger? Later, before I left his office, I detoured back. "Funny you should mention you're bipolar. My son is bipolar, too, and he's been struggling more than usual lately. Maybe it would help if he talked to you? Would you mind?"

The man smiled. And in that very moment I realized why we'd taken the detour. It was so obvious now, but in the beginning of our conversation, I hadn't a clue.

My mother told me the day before she died that what was really important in life was love. It was a strange sentiment to hear her convey because my mother had a hard time showing her love. But somehow at the end, she must have gotten a glimpse of what I saw and felt the other night.

It's four in the morning. Paul, my grandson, is in All Children's Hospital and I'm spending the night with him. There are four cribs in the room, each one has a baby in it, and there's a mom, dad, or grandparent like me sitting in the chair beside it. I've never been comfortable sharing a room with anyone, but this evening, even though we're all strangers, instantly there's a bond. Each one of us is hoping to hear good news when the doctors make their rounds in the morning. Each one of us is hoping nothing bad happens during the night.

There are curtains between the cribs, but there's really no privacy. You can't help but overhear. Across the room a husky man is leaning over a crib whispering to his four-month-old daughter, "Don't worry, honey, Daddy will always take care of you." And then he rings for the nurse, because Daddy's trying to figure out how to safely give his baby girl a hug. She just had a tumor removed from her brain and he doesn't want to hurt her.

strawberries, we walked through the flower section and that's when I got a case of the "remember when" blues. Looking at the spring flowers made me think about my father and our Easter tradition.

Every year on the day before Easter, my father would walk down to the florist, and when he came back home, he was carrying two small white boxes. Inside one was an orchid corsage for my mother, and in the other a pretty pink and white carnation corsage for me.

My father wasn't a sentimental man—far from it. He never said "I love you," but once a year when the tulips and daffodils of spring were peeking up through the ground—signaling a change in season—briefly there'd be a change in my father, too. I'm not sure how or where my dad got the idea, but buying a corsage for Mom and me became an Easter tradition.

"Look at what my dad bought for me." I wore my corsage all day long, even after I came home from church and changed into my play clothes, and I fell asleep with it on my pillow, too. When I was older and moved out on my own, my father stopped buying an Easter corsage for me. I missed it. Not just the flowers, but the way I felt every year when my father handed me the box from the florist.

Now here I was standing in the middle of the market, tears in my eyes, and my husband knew why. "I think you need some fresh flowers for Easter, Suzanne, don't these tulips look like spring?" And he handed me a pink and yellow bouquet of tulips—a new beginning and a new tradition of love.

Stories can kind of sneak up on me. When I'm writing, eventually there comes a part in the process where I become agitated and it's not clear what I'm feeling, but I plow through anyway and magically, twenty or thirty minutes later the story appears. I'm not quite sure where it came from, in fact, sometimes when I go back the next day and reread what I've written, I'm amazed I wrote it. Just where did these words, where did this ability to write come from?

Maybe I shouldn't be questioning my abilities. But as soon as I finished writing that sentence, I remembered what my mother said when I told her I was publishing a business magazine—I clearly remember the look on her face. It was a look of confusion and amazement, shock, really, and then she asked, "Just where did you learn how to do all of this?"

It was as if nothing great was expected from me, and my mother still couldn't believe I'd accomplished such a thing, or that I was successful. But truth be told, sometimes even today I stand back and look at what I do and I too wonder . . . just where and how did I learn these things?

Maybe my writing career started in high school, at least that's what some of my old school friends tell me. (They insist I used to rewrite their papers—though I have no recollection.) Then again, maybe it was the dozens of thank-you letters my mother made me write when I was a kid—I do remember those.

Guilt and my mother taught me at a very early age to always send a thank-you—immediately. Even to this day, as soon as I finish opening a gift, I hear my mother's voice: "Susan, sit down and write a thank-you note and do it this minute or you'll forget!"

A syllabus accompanied each thank-you writing assignment in our house; the thank-you needed to be at least twenty-eight words, including adjectives and sincerity. Not that I had to fake being genuinely grateful when someone gave me a gift, but when you're a kid, writing a thank-you note interferes with *actually* playing with the gift you're so thankful for. So it always seemed to me like a simple thank-you would suffice. "Thank you for the new doll. As soon as I finish this thank you note I'm going to play with it, so . . . gotta go . . . thank you. Susan Tindell."

There it was—twenty-eight words including my name.

But the toughest writing assignment I faced was a thank-you note for the white socks my aunt sent to me every year for Christmas. I realized it was the thought that counted—my mother had drilled that into me—but what could you say about a pair of white socks, year after year? At least "white" counted as one of my required adjectives.

"Thank you for the great white socks. I've never seen such bright, white socks. Those white socks will go with anything, and the handy thing about white socks is that you don't have to worry about matches. One white sock is pretty much like the next white sock. And if I forget to put my shoes on and run outside with my white socks on, Mom has a new bleach that will get the dirt out, and the socks will be white again. Thank you for the white socks."

Eighty-nine words—count 'em. More than I needed, and apparently the extra words were a little too encouraging and heartfelt, because my aunt kept sending those darn white socks.

Kid stuff aside, it's taken a long time for me to acknowledge my writing ability and actually call myself a writer. I wrote a monthly "Sorry We're Closed" column when I published *In Business* magazine, but I wasn't "really" a writer. Couldn't even bring myself to use my name and the word writer in the same sentence. Even when I decided to write a feature article about grief in the workplace, I still felt like I was pretending. Maybe with good reason. Because when I sat down to type up my notes from three different interviews, I realized I didn't know anything about using quotation marks.

Old-fashioned common sense is the first approach I try when I have a problem, and I admire other people who use the same no-frills approach. One of my favorite examples is how NASA spent bundles of money and time developing a pen that would write upside down in space. The Russians sent their crew up with pencils. So my commonsense approach for learning how to use quotation marks involved taking a bubble bath and reading *Time* magazine.

I couldn't go to the library and research the topic (my article was due in the morning), and since I needed a bath anyway and *Time* magazine was filled with oodles of direct quotes framed with those two little squiggles on each side, I filled up the tub with steaming hot water, added a capful of my favorite lavender bubbles, grabbed a yellow highlighter, and carefully skimmed the articles in my husband's copy of *Time*, noting the various placement of quotation marks. Then I matched the type of sentences I'd highlighted to the ones I'd written in my article and violà . . . I looked respectable, actually better than respectable. My final draft was barely touched by the editor's pen—and you can *quote* me on that!

In my mind I was just doing this writing thing for fun. Even when I started writing a daily column for the Dear Reader book clubs, I didn't think of myself as a writer, but other people disagreed. "Look out, Dave Barry," an executive from Penguin wrote after he finished reading a tale about my husband's boating escapades, and then a few days later he emailed again. My "Cashier for a Day" column had brought back memories of his first job in a supermarket. You might think I would have been grinning ear to ear from the compliments. I wasn't. Instead I was freaking out. *Oh my God, people are really reading this stuff, people think I'm a writer, and this guy works at a publishing house. How am I going to write tomorrow's column? This guy might be reading it!*

It took three weeks for me to shake loose the "writer" label, and just when things were getting back to normal, wouldn't you know it, a newspaper columnist contacted me. He loved my online book club concept at DearReader.com and wanted to write a story about it, and oh yeah, he loved the columns I wrote every day, too. In fact, he enjoyed my column so much, he suggested I should write it on the weekend, too.

These people were really messing with my mind. *Yes, I'm a writer . . . no, I'm not a writer . . . just pretending I'm a writer.* I thought I'd kept my multiple personality oddity pretty well camouflaged, but suddenly I felt so anxiety ridden and ashamed I could barely even write.

"When the student is ready, the teacher appears" is the wise old adage. My version: When the girl is ready to come out of the writing closet, but she needs a little coaxing, two teachers and a nosy guy at Starbucks suddenly appear.

A friend and I were sitting in Starbucks drinking coffee when a man walked over to our table. "I couldn't help but overhear your conversation, you were talking about deadlines. Are you a writer?"

The guy was looking at me, waiting for an answer. "Well, yeah, I kind of write this thing every day, um, I do these book clubs, I rarely write about books, it's kind of, well sort of, you see, I don't really (breathe, Suzanne, breathe) . . . why did you want to know?" By this time I'm sure the guy thought, *This is some weird woman*, because he slowly backed away from the table and offered a sympathetic good-bye.

People were staring—how embarrassing! This was ridiculous. What the heck was wrong with me? I really needed to work this out once and for all. *Are you a writer, Suzanne? What's the big deal? Why does this "writer" label bother you so much?*

The final confrontation came when the editor of *Working Mother* magazine called saying she'd read my column about Mrs. Creswick's Meat Loaf, "loved it," and "would I be interested in writing a monthly column for the magazine?" *Okay, Suzanne, this is your moment. Are you a writer? Can you at least tell yourself you're a writer so you can accept this project? Tell yourself you're a writer, start acting like a writer, and pretty soon even you will believe it.* And now, finally . . . I do.

My strength in life comes from my insecurities. Eventually I do find my way. It might take me longer than the average Joe, but I've never regretted the journey. Stumbling along through the uncertainty of it all, I learn so much when I'm not sure about anything. I write down the recipes from my life so I can reread them when I need confirmation. Even though the situation might look bad, I've trudged through before and I'll make it this time, too.

I have just enough confidence in myself and just enough doubt to write about my worries and fears, to make fun of myself, and invite people to laugh along with me. Wouldn't it be wonderful if we could all feel comfortable enough to laugh at ourselves when we screw up? A laughter that stays with us, tucked away inside, instead of feeling shame? Hopefully when people read the words I write they'll go easier on themselves and find that soft place to fall.

My father-in-law came over to our house for a barbecue, walked into the kitchen, said hello, and then out of the blue he commented, "You know, Suzanne, I've always wondered why you bare your innermost thoughts in the column you write every day, but now I think I understand. You make it all right for people to be themselves, whatever that might be. I imagine it's reassuring for your readers to think *Suzanne's been afraid and scared to death of life—I'm not the only one.* Or if someone feels like doing something a bit on the wild and crazy side, that's okay, too—because you've written about walking down Main Street with a bubble machine, so they know there's someone out there who's nuttier than they are."

I don't know if my father-in-law realized it, but his comments just about made me cry. Wouldn't it be wonderful if reading my column put someone at ease? Nothing would make me happier. I've spent way too much of my life worrying, *Am I doing it right?* and it was such a relief such a big relief—when I finally accepted the fact that there *are* a lot of times when I don't do life the way most people do it, but that's okay. I used to spend so much time imitating other folks and trying to get them to like me that I forgot to spend time getting to like myself. I hope I never forget it's okay to be me—whoever that might be.

The more I write, the more I learn about myself. It's a love/hate sort of thing. Writing keeps me honest. Every day I hold up a mirror and force myself to look in it—sometimes I try to resist what I see. Sometimes I can barely breathe when I'm writing. That's when I know I've found the thing I need to write about. Interesting, isn't it? When I can't breathe and feel like I might pass out any minute, then I know I've come face-to-face with the boogeyman hiding underneath my bed. Learning about me is so exciting. Where else could I get this kind of thrill for free?

Writing has taught me that simpler is better. Take it easy, slow down, Suzanne, and simply say what's on your mind. Maybe I should use impressive words, sonorous adjectives, or make the sentences complex. But writing isn't really any different from other things in life. Too much eye shadow—what *was* I thinking? The first Dove Bar tasted divine, so I ate another—my stomach rebelled. The man at the deli thought he was doing me a favor when he put a little bit more of everything on my sandwich, but it was too much.

When life gets to be too much and I don't know where to begin, I start writing. It's not easy. Fear gets in the way, but if I keep at it, eventually one single line in the midst of my jumbled thoughts is staring back at me. It feels good to read it and I realize it's the comfort I've been looking for, my soft place to fall.

What will people think? used to be the first thing I'd think about when I sat down to write, but not anymore. If I want to give my best, I need to get to the place inside of me that's a little vulnerable. It can be scary. Give a lot, put it all out there, and someone may take advantage because some people take all you have to give and give nothing back in return.

But it's worth the risk—giving a little bit of myself—because readers give the nicest, most meaningful gifts back. Readers share a story, maybe one that hasn't come to mind for years. A story about the funny thing that happened when their grandfather was still alive, they remember—and I feel their laughter in between the lines they've written. Or maybe it's a confession, something they needed to say out loud, so they could ease their pain. I hear them crying and in a reply I reassure them there are times when none of us does the right thing, including me, and silently we cry together.

Years ago, Ann, a reader at my book clubs, sent an email, and before she signed off, Ann closed with these words: "You take good care."

I can't explain it, but those simple words continue to stay with me. Every time I think about them I feel loved and cared for and I'm right back in Mrs. Creswick's kitchen. I've never met Ann, but the words she wrote rescued me again just the other day. Everything I tried to do was a struggle. Nothing was going right and then I heard Ann whispering, "You take good care."

It's the kind of good-bye that's not an ending, but a blessing. I don't know where your life's journey is right now, or where it will take you, but I wish you well. *"You take good care."*

Thanks for reading with me. It's so good to read with friends.

One Last Note from the Author

It truly was a boy-meets-girl love story. The girl was in her early seventies, the boy in his late sixties. My mother and Ron had a magical first date and were married just a few months later. But the happily-ever-after part of the story lasted only a short time. One year and eight months after they were married, my mother died from lung cancer.

Ron never stopped loving and pining for my mother. Frequently he'd call to talk, reliving stories about the things they did together. Nothing fancy, just simple things like the time they sat together on a bench looking out over the water while a light mist of rain was falling, or the flower garden Ron planted in the backyard for my mother. A flower garden he still lovingly tended. "When I'm in the garden, it feels like your mother is right beside me." And each time Ron would call, before he'd say good-bye, the tears would flow. Oh, how he missed my mother.

In 2008, three years after Mom passed away, Ron also was diagnosed with lung cancer. He continued to call and reminisce about my mother, but he also started asking, "When is your book going to be finished, Suzanne? I don't know how much longer I'll be around."

On a Thursday afternoon in August 2009, Ron's son called to tell me that hospice was on the way and funeral arrangements were being made for his father. My book was still in production, so I carefully wrapped a copy of my manuscript in tissue paper tied with a ribbon and sent it overnight to Ron's home.

You don't die alone when you live in a small town. There was a steady flow of family, friends, and neighbors stopping by to say good-bye, and everyone who sat a spell read a little bit of my manuscript to Ron.

Sunday afternoon my phone rang and it was Ron. "Suzanne, I've called to give you the first review of your book. It's wonderful. Reading your book was the last entry on the list of things I wanted to accomplish, so now it's time to go and be with your mother."

Ron passed away early the next morning on Monday, August 17, 2009.

Writing it down this moment, it sounds a little like a fairy tale. But in a strange sort of way I do believe it was one of those true love stories, and that my mother and Ron are finally together again, happily ever after.

Ron's on the left, my mother's on the right, and that's me in the middle holding a big, ugly bowl. Just one of the many "finds" they came home with on their daily Florida garage-sale escapades.

Acknowledgments

I dedicate this book to my loving husband, Bob; I'm one lucky woman. The longer we're married, the more in love I am with you.

Writing a book was hard work and I never would have succeeded if it hadn't been for a group of friends and an agent who believed in me, even before I did. Thank you for hanging in there with me.

"Take as much time as you need." Those words gave me permission to grieve as long as I needed after my mother died, and those same words gave me permission to take as much time as I needed to write this book. Thank you, M. J. Rose, for being there every step of the way; I'm such a lucky woman. You've been a cherished friend and mentor since the first day we met in New York City.

"How can I make the transition?" I'd been a daily columnist for ten years, so in the beginning, when I'd sit down to start writing this book, I'd end up writing a column instead. "You can do it and I'll help you." Thank you, Sully (Thomas Sullivan), for the long-distance tutoring.

(What a Feeling)," she does just that—except she accidentally winds up with an audience. Have you ever experienced a similar situation? Was it comical like Suzanne's, or more embarrassing?

5. When describing her own quirky personality, Suzanne quotes Leonard Cohen's "There's a crack in everything. That's how the light gets in." How do you think Suzanne's embracing of her individuality and pride in being "a little strange" (page 74) has affected the way she interacts with others? How can embracing one's uniqueness help overcome life's obstacles?

6. An illness or injury can be one of life's biggest setbacks. Suzanne experienced such a setback when she was diagnosed with benign essential blepharospasm, a rare, incurable neurological disorder. Determined to overcome her disability, Suzanne learned to love her illness in order to live with it. Do you think her "love the illness" strategy could help others suffering from chronic conditions? Have you ever experienced a similar situation? If so, how did you learn to live with your condition?

7. In talking about the meaning of life, Suzanne writes, "I've always thought my job, my purpose here on earth, certainly must be something more dramatic than simply loving and taking care of the people around me. So I've strived to be clever, artistic, and talented in business. But . . . I realize I've been looking at life all wrong. It's not complicated, there's nothing to prove. My mother was right. It's really very simple. What's really important is love." Do you agree? Why or why not?

8. After her mom passed away, Suzanne discovered a short poem that her grandmother had given to her mother. The poem is just a silly anti-theft ditty written on an index card, but she cherishes the keepsake and makes an index card of her own because, as she says, "[S]ometimes a little bit of silliness is the recipe I need to get me through the day" (pages 78–79). Of all the values Suzanne carries, why do you think maintaining a sense of humor is so important? Are there any special pick-me-up tokens or rituals in your life that you use to help you through rough patches?

9. One of the book's main themes is family traditions. Holiday traditions are particularly important to Suzanne, so much so that she has trouble parting with antiquated rituals like buying pecan pies at Christmas. She also recognizes the importance of maintaining traditions now that she's responsible for holiday dinners. How important is tradition in your family? Did you experience a similar "passing of the torch" when you became an adult?

10. For a long time Suzanne was ambivalent about going home to visit her parents, even to the point of becoming physically ill. But through Mrs. Creswick's meat loaf and other recipes and stories from her recipe box, Suzanne discovered a way to go back home. What does going home mean to you? Has it been an easy journey or, like Suzanne, have you had to find a way to give yourself the home you never had when you were growing up?

11. Suzanne recounts the day when she was sitting in Starbucks and a man came over to her table and asked, "Are you a writer" (page 224)? After stumbling through an

awkward and embarrassing response, Suzanne realized it was finally time to face her moment of truth. Was she going to accept and acknowledge her writing talent, or let self-doubt continue to steal it away? The words in an old folk song proclaim, "This little light of mine, I'm going to let it shine." Have you been able to freely acknowledge the talents you've been blessed with, or do you hide your light under a bushel?

12. Toward the end of the book, Suzanne writes about having the courage to "deviate from my comfortable routine" in order to discover new opportunities to touch other people's lives (page 216). So many of her projects required her to trust her instincts and take a chance. For example, when she took it upon herself to essentially create her own job description at Sunny Hill Nursing Home. Have you ever found yourself in situations where you had an opportunity to take similar chances, and how did you react? Do you regret your decision?

A Conversation with Suzanne Beecher

You end your book with the same line you end your blog posts and website entries, "Thanks for reading with me. It's so good to read with friends." Is there a special significance to this phrase?

When you grow up in a small town like I did, the feeling of belonging to a community of friends comes naturally. Whenever I'd go for a walk, or ride my bike down the street, frequently I'd stop to say hello to a neighbor. So even though more than 365,000 people read at my book clubs every day, when I'm working on my column it feels like I'm writing to one single person. Just sitting at the kitchen table, drinking coffee, and chatting with a friend. The ending for my column, "Thanks for reading with me. It's so good to read with friends," wasn't planned. It's simply the sentiment this small-town girl feels in her heart each day when she finishes writing her column.

In the preface of Muffins and Mayhem, *you write about how you have only four childhood memories. Did writing your book help you recapture any additional memories, or do you still draw a blank when the topic of childhood memories comes up in conversation?*

Writing *Muffins and Mayhem* definitely helped me recall other childhood memories. Antique stores have become another trigger for helping me remember the past. Whenever my husband and I walk through one, he's amazed at how many times I'll see something and comment, "Ah, look at that! It looks just like the one Grandma Hale used to have in her kitchen." Every old cookie jar, potato ricer, or serving bowl for sale, reminds me of another childhood memory that I'd tucked deep away.

You've had a range of jobs, from publisher of In Business *to volunteer coordinator at Sunny Hill Nursing Home. Which one of your past jobs is your favorite? Why?*

That's easy. Meals for Madison, my free lunch program in Madison, Wisconsin. My life was in crisis when I started the meal program. *In Business* magazine was losing huge amounts of money, so in a way it was kind of crazy for me to start a program that gives away free food.

Yet I knew in my heart I was doing exactly what I was supposed to be doing. The lesson I learned from the meal program is that helping other people with their problems also helps me with my own. Meals for Madison didn't solve my financial problems with the magazine, but the experience of helping someone else brought joy and peace into my life. Now, whenever I'm consumed with my own problems, I'm reminded it's time to do something for someone else.

In Muffins and Mayhem *you talk about the importance of role models and the impact Mrs. Creswick, one of your role models, had on your life. Can you think of another adult figure from your childhood who was as influential as Mrs. Creswick?*

Two people immediately come to mind: Grandma Hale and Andy Griffith. I realize mentioning my grandmother probably doesn't come as a surprise, but why Andy Griffith?

Mayberry, the town depicted in the Andy Griffith television show, was much like the one I grew up in, and Andy Griffith was the father I wished I had. To this day, watching reruns of the *Andy Griffith Show* while I'm cooking is one of my favorite pastimes. I think I know the story line of every single episode by heart, but that's okay, because it makes Mayberry feel even more like home to me.

I spent a lot of time at my Grandma Hale's house when I was young, and even though Grandma was on the quiet side, she cared for me as I always wished my own mother would have. It's the little things that stand out in my mind. At my house when I wasn't feeling well, my mother actually got angry with me, sort of suggesting somehow it was my fault that I was sick. So I was pretty much left to take care of myself. But if I wasn't feeling well at Grandma's house, things were different. I remember one time when I was visiting Grandma and I was up in the middle of the night sick to my stomach and throwing up, Grandma Hale loved me anyway and never left my side all night long.

You and your husband have collaborated on numerous projects and business endeavors throughout your relationship. Do you still work closely together now that DearReader.com has become so successful? How have the time demands of running the online book club and blog affected your business partnership?

My husband and I continue to work together, and we couldn't imagine it any other way. But we don't work on the exact same project—that's a bit too close. I think my husband and I work well together because we trust each other completely. Consequently, we never feel like we're in competition, but rather a working team. Of course, sometimes our relationship does get off course, and when that happens the sentence that brings harmony back into our conversation is, "We've been here before, let's start again." It's our cue to reevaluate the dynamics of what's really going on.

You talk very candidly about learning to live with benign essential blepharospasm, and how you learned to love your illness. Do you still have a good relationship with BEB? Can you offer any advice for others who are currently learning to love their own illnesses?

Yes, my disorder and I are still buddies, but we continue to discover new things about each other's personalities. In some ways my eye disorder is kind of like living with a roommate. I'm an only child who still prefers her own space, so periodically my BEB and I get into a disagreement. My eyes get tired, my nervous system needs a nap, but Suzanne wants to keep going. I'm upset that I can't do what I want, when I want, so I say some unkind words about how my stupid eye disorder slows me down. But my "roommate" doesn't appreciate my choice of words, or my stubbornness. So my disorder retaliates with a one-two punch in return, which completely drains my energy, and then I have no choice but to rest in bed for a couple of days. Eventually we both come to our senses and negotiate a way to live peacefully together again.

If there's one personality trait that readers of Muffins and Mayhem *learn about you, it's your entrepreneurial spirit. Do you have plans in the works for any future projects outside your DearReader.com program?*
I've never planned any of my new business ventures; opportunities just seemed to show up and I simply jumped on board. So I don't have any plans at the moment, other than to continue creating new ideas for my online book clubs, and I'd like to become more personally involved with libraries around the country. I do have plans for a second book. But as far as launching another new business venture, I think I may have exchanged some of my entrepreneurial spirit with the desire to spend more time with my four grandchildren. I'm amazed at how they've affected me. I have such fond memories of the time I spent with my Grandma and Grandpa Hale, and I sure hope I'm creating those kinds of memories for my grandchildren, too.

You run multiple websites, including the DearReader.com book club and your own blog. Have you always been so web-savvy? Do you have any advice for someone just starting a blog or web-based business?
My website is one of the survivors from the early Internet boom, when folks had the attitude, "If you build it, they will come—and you don't have to worry about making money." That kind of thinking remains a mystery to me. I guess I'm old-school, because to me it doesn't matter where the business is located—you need to have customers and you need to find a way to make money. If you're going to start a web-based business, don't quit your day job until your new business is bringing in income. Having said that, I do believe if you love what you do, the money will follow—at least enough money to live a joyful life.

What's your favorite recipe in Muffins and Mayhem*?*
Skunk Beans. This is going to sound a little strange, but whenever I make Skunk Beans, I remember as a kid singing this little ditty:

Beans, beans, the musical fruit
The more you eat, the more you toot.
The more you toot, the better you feel,
So eat more beans with every meal!

Pork 'n' Beans were frequently on the dinner table when I was a kid. After saying grace and before we started eating, I'd sing the bean song out loud. Each line with a little more emphasis than the last, so by the time I reached the crescendo at the end of the song, my arms were waving high up in the air and I'd be laughing. There wasn't a lot of laughing in my house when I was a kid, so the little girl inside of me loves the Skunk Beans recipe the most. But not to worry, these beans are toot-proof! That confirmation comes from experience, because I've served these beans to my family for years and we've never had a toot outbreak yet!

How different was the process of writing Muffins and Mayhem *from your online writing? Do you prefer book writing to writing your daily blog column?*
There's an art to writing a column for the DearReader.com book clubs because space is limited, and in my case there's a daily deadline. The ideal number of words is 360. That's not a lot of words when your goal is to tell a story, including a laugh or a tear that you hope will touch someone's heart, and then wrap it all up neatly in the end. I love what I do, but it's a pretty big assignment every day. Since I only have a few words to tell a story in my column, there's not much sauntering allowed. I have to stay on track with my original idea. But in a book, there's room to wander, as long as it's an interesting journey. I don't know how most authors approach a book, but since it was all new to me, I had no choice but to let the book take charge. I can honestly say that I never knew for sure what I was doing until it was all over. Looking back I'm amazed at where some of the chapters took me. Writing a book was a magical journey for me and I'm ready to begin again.

Enhance Your Book Club

1. Plan a book club smorgasbord! Have everyone prepare his or her favorite recipe either from the book or from Suzanne's recipe blog (DearReader.com) and bring it to your book club meeting. Or prepare one of your family's favorite recipes and share the story behind it.
2. One of the most inspiring experiences Suzanne writes about is her role as volunteer coordinator. Give back to your own community by volunteering in your neighborhood.
3. Visit the author's website, DearReader.com, and see firsthand how Suzanne's free online book clubs work!
4. Visit Suzanne's website MuffinsandMayhem.com, and create a cookbook of recipes and stories with your reading group or family members, or make one for yourself.

Printed in the United States
By Bookmasters